FELON TO FORTUNE

The Billionaire Barbie Blueprint

How I Turned Trauma into Triumph and Hustle into a Financial Empire

BY BILLIONAIRE BARBIE

DISCLAIMER

The advice contained in this material might not be suitable for everyone. The author designed the information to present her opinion about the subject matter. The reader must carefully investigate all aspects of any business decision before committing to him or herself. The author obtained the information contained herein from sources she believes to be reliable and from her own personal experience, but she neither implies nor intends any guarantee of accuracy. The author is not in the business of giving legal, accounting, or any other type of professional advice. Should the reader need such advice, he or she must seek services from a competent professional. The author particularly disclaims any liability, loss, or risk taken by individuals who directly or indirectly act on the information contained herein. The author believes the advice presented here is sound, but readers cannot hold her responsible for either the actions they take, or the risk taken by individuals who directly or indirectly act on the information contained herein.

Published by 1BrickPublishing
Printed in the United States
Copyright © 2025 by Latoya Littles
ISBN 979-8898560119

DEDICATION

To every girl who was told she wouldn't make it, To every woman who had to survive when she should've been protected, To the ones who've been judged by their past and counted out by the world—This is for you.

And to the younger me, who danced in pain, loved with fear, and dreamed in silence... You didn't just survive. You built a legacy.

This blueprint is our testimony. May it remind you that your story ain't over— it's just getting started.

DEDICATION REQUEST

Please share this book with anyone who's ever felt stuck, silenced, or ashamed of their past—so they can see that redemption is real, success is possible, and their story still has power.

Table of Contents

INTRODUCTION

THE UNLIKELY MOGUL

I'm sitting on a private jet with some of the most successful Black entrepreneurs in America. Outside the window, clouds drift by like cotton candy dreams I once thought were reserved for other people—people born with silver spoons, college degrees, and clean records. Not for girls from Outeast, Jacksonville's roughest neighborhood. Not for high school dropouts. Definitely not for five-time felons who spent their 24th birthday in prison.

Yet here I am—Billionaire Barbie, building a financial empire, teaching thousands of women how to get legally rich, and creating generational wealth on my own terms.

The flight attendant offers me champagne, and as I take a sip, I flash back to another moment: sitting on a metal bunk in county jail, staring at cinderblock walls, facing 40 years for crimes that took less than 30 seconds to commit. I remember the guard calling my name for court, the cold metal of handcuffs against my wrists, and the moment the judge looked at me and reduced my sentence from ten years to seven—favor that wasn't fair but saved my life.

The contrast between these two realities isn't lost on me. In fact, it's precisely the point of this book.

This isn't a rags-to-riches fairytale where everything magically works out. I'm not some special unicorn who just got lucky. What happened between that jail cell and this private jet was a deliberate transformation—one that followed a blueprint anyone can access if they're willing to do the work, shift their mindset, and learn the rules of a game most of us were never taught.

I built my first six-figure business with no formal education, no business loans, and a felony record that should have disqualified me from most opportunities. I did it again with my second business, my third, and my fourth. Today, I run multiple seven-figure companies teaching everything from tax strategy to credit repair to content creation, and I've helped thousands of men and women—many with backgrounds similar to mine—build their own wealth.

Let me be clear about something: I'm not proud of every choice I've made. Some parts of my story are painful to share. I've been a victim. I've been a perpetrator. I've done things out of desperation, trauma, and ignorance that hurt others and nearly destroyed me. But I refuse to let shame silence me, because my story—even the ugly parts—might be the blueprint someone else needs.

In these pages, I'm going to tell you exactly how I did it—how I went from dancing in strip clubs at 14 to building businesses that create financial freedom. I'll show you how I turned my street hustle into legitimate entrepreneurship, transformed my prison time into business strategy, and leveraged my trauma into my greatest strength.

This book is different from other business or motivational books you might have read. It's raw. It's real. I'm not going to sugarcoat the struggle or pretend I didn't make devastating mistakes. I'm going to tell you about the time I lost a quarter-million dollars in three days, the relationship decisions that nearly bankrupted me, and the painful lessons I had to learn repeatedly before they stuck.

But this isn't just my testimony. It's your blueprint.

Each chapter of my journey contains actionable lessons you can apply to your own life, whether you're starting from rock bottom or just feeling stuck in a life that's too small for your dreams. At the end of each chapter, you'll find "Blueprint Lessons" or "Boss Tips"—concrete strategies I've used to build wealth, heal from trauma, and create the life I once only fantasized about during long nights in a prison cell.

You might be wondering why I'm sharing all this. Why would someone who's "made it" expose the messiest parts of their past? The truth is, I'm tired of seeing women who look like me, who come from places like mine, who've survived what I survived, struggling paycheck to paycheck while watching others build generational wealth. I'm tired of seeing people with criminal records believe their past defines their future. I'm tired of watching talented, resilient women dim their light because society told them they don't deserve to shine.

When I was at my lowest, I promised God that if He got me out, I would become a vessel—that I would use whatever platform I was given to bring others with me. This book is part of fulfilling that promise.

So whether you're reading this in a prison cell, a shelter, a corporate office you hate, or a place of transition where you're trying to figure out what's next—this book is for you. I'm writing to the woman who knows she's capable of more but doesn't know where to start. I'm writing to the formerly incarcerated person trying to rebuild their life. I'm writing to the hustler looking to legitimize their skills and the dreamer afraid to put pen to paper.

Your background is not your destiny. Your mistakes are not your identity. Your trauma can become your triumph if you let it. And the very things society told you would keep you broke, burdened, and broken can become your greatest business assets.

I know because I lived it.

Turn the page, and let me show you how.

— Billionaire Barbie

PART I:
THE FOUNDATION -
JACKSONVILLE ROOTS

CHAPTER 1

OUTEAST MADE ME
- GROWING UP BARBIE

"**W**hat happens in this house, stays in this house."

That was the unwritten rule in every home in Outeast, the neighborhood in Jacksonville, Florida, where I spent my early years. It wasn't just a saying—it was survival code. In communities like mine, silence protected the family, even when that silence was slowly killing us.

I didn't know Outeast was considered the worst part of Jacksonville until I was older. To little Barbie, it was just home—a big, crowded house on Spearing Street filled with family, food, and all the contradictions that come with growing up Black in America.

Our house was the gathering place, the heartbeat of the family. My grandmother Mozell Stanley—born August 10, 1941, a war baby with the fighting spirit to match—ruled that house with an iron will and boundless love. My grandfather, her partner of 45 years, showed me my first example of a man who provided. My mother Barbara (yes, I got my name from her, though she'll tell you I stole it), my aunties, uncles, and cousins—we all lived together, breathing the same air, sharing the same struggles, celebrating the same small victories.

Weekends meant crab boils, Florida-style with blue crab, shrimp, and crawfish that would make your mouth water just smelling it from down the block. Fish fries. Barbecues. Music. Laughter. We'd play flag football in the streets with no shoes, our bare feet tough enough to handle the hot pavement. We'd ride our bicycles blocks and blocks away, chain breaking, knees bleeding, freedom flowing through our veins.

"Baby, don't go too far," my grandma would call out, but "too far" was relative in a neighborhood where kids had free range. No helicopter parenting back then—we were community raised, street smart by necessity.

What I didn't understand then, but see clearly now, is that poverty has a way of creating its own beauty. When you don't have much, you make everything count. You turn nothing into something. You find joy in small moments because big opportunities aren't knocking on your door.

My grandmother taught me resilience. She was a hustler who didn't have to hustle—my grandpa provided everything—but she still found ways to make her own money. "Never wait on nobody," she'd say, echoing what would later become my mother's mantra to me. I'd watch her cook, clean, handle business, then start a side hustle just because she could. She showed me that a woman shouldn't depend on anyone, even when she has someone dependable.

She also taught me to stand up for myself. I was always fighting in school—girls especially had it out for me—and my grandma would ride up to the school on her beach cruiser to make sure nobody jumped me.

"You're gonna see her one-on-one," she'd tell them, all five feet nothing of her, facing down girls twice her size. My grandmother didn't play about her grandbaby. She was the first person who made me feel protected in a world that often felt dangerous.

My mother was beautiful—a real-life Barbie doll to me—but complex in ways I couldn't understand as a child. She worked two, sometimes three jobs to make ends meet. She always made sure I was fly, even if it meant making sacrifices. Priorities, you know? In the hood, appearance is currency. It's respect. It's sometimes the only thing you control.

I would sit and watch her get ready—putting on makeup, doing her hair, transforming herself—and I was mesmerized. In those moments, I saw power. The power to be beautiful despite circumstances. The power to command attention. The power to be seen in a world that often renders Black women invisible.

But beauty and strength weren't the only things I inherited from my mother. There was also the rage. The inability to handle conflict without explosion. The screaming, the cursing, the chaos that felt normal because it was all I knew. My mom and grandma would butt heads constantly, two strong Black women with nowhere to channel their pain except at each other.

I didn't know it then, but we were living out generational patterns—patterns of both strength and dysfunction that would shape who I became.

Until I was about nine or ten, my life felt like a normal childhood—tough around the edges, but full of love, food, family, and freedom. I was happy in the way children are happy when they don't know any different. I was loved fiercely, if imperfectly. I was provided for, even when providing meant sacrifice.

Then came the day everything changed.

I was sexually molested by someone very close to me—someone I trusted, someone who should have protected me. I won't name them here, not because I'm protecting them, but because this part of my story is about what violation does to a child, not about exposing someone for actions they may or may not have faced consequences for.

I didn't understand what was happening to me. I knew it felt wrong, dangerous, confusing. I knew instinctively that it was something I shouldn't tell anyone about—partly because of that "what happens in this house stays in this house" mentality, and partly because in communities like mine, predators were often protected while victims were silenced.

I didn't speak about it until I was 21 years old. That's how deep the silence went. That's how thoroughly I had internalized the message that my pain didn't deserve a voice.

What I didn't realize then—couldn't have possibly understood—was how that moment would ripple through every aspect of my life. How it would affect the way I viewed myself, men, money, and power. How it would drive me to seek validation in dangerous ways. How it would push me toward self-destruction before I finally found self-creation.

In the hood, trauma isn't treated—it's normalized. It's not "what happened to you," it's just "what happens." Everyone's got a story. Everyone's carrying weight. You learn to move with it, through it, despite it. You learn to wear your damage like armor, or you don't survive.

I learned early that the world wasn't safe, that the people closest to you could hurt you worst, and that a girl in my position had limited options for escape. I didn't have therapy. I didn't have healing spaces. I had the streets, I had my wits, and eventually, I had a desperate need to get away by any means necessary.

When I look back at little Barbie—that girl with skinned knees and big dreams, watching her mama get ready and wishing to be just like her—I see now what she couldn't see then. I see how the foundation of my empire was being laid in the most unlikely of places: in trauma, in struggle, in the unspoken codes of a neighborhood that taught me to hustle before I even knew what hustling was.

The first real "successful" people I ever saw were the drug dealers in my neighborhood. They had the cars, the clothes, the jewelry, the respect. When adults asked what I wanted to be when I grew up, I'd say, "I want to be like him"—pointing at the man on the corner with money in his pocket and power in his posture. Not his girlfriend. Him. The one in charge. The one who didn't ask for permission.

I didn't know I was pointing at death or prison. I just knew I was pointing at freedom. At escape. At a version of success that seemed attainable when all other versions felt like fairytales meant for other children.

My obsession with Barbie dolls started around this time, too—another irony that wouldn't become clear until much later. My mother bought me every Barbie doll I wanted, and I was captivated by this plastic woman who had everything: the dream house, the cars, the clothes, the career, the lifestyle. In my mind, Barbie wasn't just a toy—she was the blueprint for a life beyond Spearing Street. She had options. She had agency. She had nice things without having to depend on anybody.

"I want to be just like Barbie," I'd tell my mother, who probably thought it was cute. She didn't realize I was creating a vision board with those plastic dolls. She didn't know I was planting seeds that would eventually grow into my identity, my brand, my future.

Years later, when the Barbie movie premiered on my birthday (July 21) and made a billion dollars at the box office, headlines would read "Billionaire Barbie"—and I'd feel a chill of recognition. God has a wild sense of humor sometimes.

But before I could become Billionaire Barbie, I had to survive being Barbie from Outeast. I had to navigate the aftermath of violation, the limitations of poverty, and the danger of growing up female in an environment where girls became women far too soon.

I had to run away to find myself, even if what I found initially was more trouble.

I had to fall, repeatedly and hard, before I could rise.

And I had to learn that sometimes, your biggest pain becomes your biggest purpose—but only if you're brave enough to look at it directly, heal it intentionally, and transform it completely.

That's what this book is about. That's what my life became about. And it all started in that house on Spearing Street, where a little girl with big dreams learned that the world wasn't fair, but that didn't mean she couldn't win.

BLUEPRINT LESSON: Recognize Your Origin Story's Power

We all come from somewhere. Whether your somewhere was the projects or the suburbs, a two-parent home or the foster care system, your origin story contains both gifts and wounds that shape who you become.

The key is learning to separate what serves you from what limits you. Here's how:

1. **Identify Your Inherited Strengths**: What survival skills did your environment teach you? For me, it was hustle, resilience, and the ability to read people quickly. These translate directly to business when channeled properly.

2. **Name Your Trauma Without Shame**: Acknowledge what happened to you without letting it define you. Trauma unaddressed becomes behavior uncontrolled. When I finally spoke about my sexual abuse, it lost some of its power over my choices.

3. **Find the Hidden Lessons**: Even in dysfunction, there are teachings. My grandmother's side hustles showed me entrepreneurship before I knew the word. My mother's ability to "put on" despite circumstances taught me about image and branding.

4. **Challenge the Limiting Narratives**: What stories did your community tell about what was possible for someone like you? Identify these narratives to consciously reject them. The drug dealers seemed like the only successful model in my neighborhood, but that was a lie I had to unlearn.

5. **Rewrite Without Erasing**: Your past made you, but it doesn't have to limit you. Honor where you came from while refusing to be trapped by it. I'm still Barbie from Outeast—that will never

change—but now that identity powers my empire instead of constraining my options.

Your background isn't your destiny, but it is your differentiation in business. The very things you survived can become your superpower when you learn to leverage them instead of being leveraged by them.

CHAPTER 2

RUNNING AWAY FROM HOME, RUNNING TOWARD TROUBLE

A t 14, I had reached my breaking point with my mother.

Let me be clear about something before I go further: my mother and I are in an excellent place now. But back then, we were two wounded people hurting each other because we didn't know how to heal ourselves. She was barely 19 when she had me, which means she was literally just a girl trying to raise a girl. Looking back, I see that clearly. But at 14, all I could see was the yelling, the chaos, the feeling like I was suffocating in that house.

The sexual abuse had changed me in ways I couldn't articulate. I was angry all the time—at everyone, but especially at the people closest to me. I felt like a stranger in my own skin, like everyone could see my secret shame written across my face. The house that once felt like love now felt like a prison where I had to pretend everything was normal when nothing felt normal anymore.

My mother's conflict resolution style didn't help. We're a family of fighters—not just physically, though that happened too—but verbally. Everything was an argument. Everything was drama. We weren't the type to sweep problems under the rug, but maybe we should have swept some shit under the rug because God, it was exhausting living in constant chaos.

I watched my grandmother and mother go at it constantly. I saw how toxic our communication patterns were, how we handled disagreements with screaming and cursing instead of actual resolution. And I knew—even at 14—that I didn't want to become that. I couldn't see a way to break the cycle while living in the middle of it.

So I ran.

At first, I didn't have a plan beyond getting as far away from that house as possible. I just knew I needed space to breathe, to figure out who I was becoming without everyone's expectations and dysfunction pressing down on me. Running away seemed like the only way to find myself.

But here's what they don't tell you about running away: it costs money. A lot of money. Money I didn't have.

I was staying with friends, bouncing around, trying to figure it out. Then one weekend changed everything. I went to a regular club for the first time—just a teenager trying to feel grown, trying to escape the weight of everything I was carrying. That same weekend, one of my friends went dancing for the first time. We were both doing these "adult" things, feeling like we were finally free.

Monday came, and we compared notes. I told her about the club, the music, the feeling of being invisible in a room full of strangers. She told me about dancing—and then she showed me the money she made.

I'm talking about a stack of bills that looked like a thousand dollars to my 14-year-old eyes. More money than I'd ever seen someone my age have. More money than my mother brought home some weeks working multiple jobs.

"Wait," I said, staring at those bills. "How did you make this? What did you actually do?"

She broke it down for me. The club. The stage. The men who threw money like it was nothing. The simple equation of using what you got to get what you need.

My mind started racing. I was already running from home. I already needed money to survive on my own. And here was a solution that seemed to solve both problems at once.

I convinced my cousin to let me borrow her ID. I told her I was going to a club—which wasn't technically a lie—but I didn't tell her the whole truth about what I planned to do there. Looking back, I can't believe how easy it was for a 14-year-old to walk into an adult establishment. We lived in different times, but that doesn't make it right.

I remember getting these dance costumes but being too scared to even take my jeans off at first. I had jeans on over everything, like that would somehow make it less real, less permanent. I was terrified, but desperation is a powerful motivator.

Walking into that club for the first time was like entering an alien world. The lights, the music, the energy—it hit different than the regular club I'd been to. These women were beautiful, confident, moving their bodies like they owned the room. And men were throwing money like it was confetti.

I was in awe and terrified at the same time. Part of me was thinking, "What the fuck am I doing here? How did I get here?" But another part of me—the rebellious part that had been building since the abuse, since the constant fighting at home—was thinking, "I'm not backing down. We're going to figure this out."

I stood there taking it all in, studying these women like I was cramming for a test. How they moved, how they talked to customers, how they handled the money. I was always the type who could see ahead, who could figure out the game by watching. So I watched. I learned. And slowly, I started to understand the economics of the room.

These women had power here. Not the kind of power I'd seen at home— the power that came from screaming the loudest or being the strongest. This was different. This was power that came from desire, from controlling something men wanted. And they were getting paid for it. Well.

I'm not going to romanticize what happened next. Dancing at 14 messed with my head in ways I'm still unpacking. It taught me to view my body as a commodity before I'd even figured out who I was as a person. It introduced me to a world where manipulation and performance often meant survival.

But it also gave me something I'd never had before: financial independence. For the first time in my life, I could take care of myself. I didn't have to ask anyone for anything. I didn't have to depend on the volatile emotions and explosive fights of the adults in my life.

I learned quickly that there was an art to it. It wasn't just about being pretty or having a nice body—though those things helped. It was about reading people, understanding psychology, knowing how to make someone feel special while protecting your own emotional boundaries. It was sales, really. The product just happened to be fantasy.

Some nights I'd make more than my mother made in a month. I was 14 years old with more cash than grown women in my neighborhood. That kind of money, that kind of independence, at that age? It changes you. It made me feel powerful in a world that had made me feel powerless. But it also disconnected me from the normal teenage experience, from the chance to develop healthy relationships with money, with men, with my own body.

The older I got, the more I understood that this wasn't sustainable. I could see women in their thirties still dancing, and to my teenage mind, thirty seemed ancient. I used to think, "I am NOT going to be thirty in somebody's club." And I wasn't—I spoke that into existence. But at 14, with limited options and unlimited bills, dancing felt like my only way out.

What I know now that I didn't know then is that running away from one problem often leads you straight into another. I was trying to escape the dysfunction at home, but I ran toward a different kind of dysfunction— one that paid well but cost even more.

The money was real. The independence was real. But so was the damage. I was learning to use my sexuality as currency before I even understood my own sexuality. I was developing survival skills that would serve me in business later, but also trauma responses that would sabotage my relationships for years.

During this time, I started to see clear patterns about money and power. The men in these clubs had money because they had legitimate businesses, careers, education. They could afford to throw hundreds of dollars at entertainment because they made thousands in their regular lives. Meanwhile, I was making good money, but it was tied to my physical presence, my youth, my willingness to perform.

I began to understand that there were different levels to this money game. There was survival money—what I was making. And there was wealth money—what they had. I wanted to graduate from one to the other, but I didn't know how yet.

The clubs also taught me about image and branding before I knew those words. The most successful dancers weren't always the most beautiful—they were the most memorable. They had personalities, stories, ways of making customers feel special. They understood that repeat business came from connection, not just attraction.

I started applying this psychology outside the club too. I learned how to read rooms, how to mirror energy, how to make people comfortable. These skills would later become invaluable in business, but they came at the cost of learning to be authentically myself.

For about nine years, on and off, dancing was my hustle. Some periods I'd be more active, other times I'd try to step away and find something else. But whenever I needed money fast—really fast—I knew where to go. It was my backup plan, my safety net, my way of controlling my financial destiny when everything else felt out of control.

The independence it gave me was intoxicating, but so was the lifestyle. I thought I was winning, but I was actually losing pieces of myself I wouldn't even know were missing until much later.

Looking back, I understand now that I was trying to gain control over my life the only way I knew how. The sexual abuse had made me feel powerless, like my body belonged to someone else. Dancing gave me a way to reclaim ownership, to profit from male desire instead of being victimized by it. It was twisted logic, but it was the best logic I had at the time.

I also understand now that I was repeating generational patterns in new ways. My grandmother hustled because she wanted to, even though she didn't have to. My mother worked multiple jobs to survive. I was hustling too, just in a different arena. The common thread was the refusal to depend on anyone else for our survival. Independent at any cost.

What I didn't realize was how much this early relationship with money would shape everything that came after. I learned that money equals freedom, that physical assets (including your body) could generate income, and that traditional paths weren't for girls like me anyway. Some of these lessons would serve me well in business. Others would nearly destroy me.

But all of them were necessary steps on the path to who I'd eventually become.

Because here's what I know for sure: every experience, even the ones that hurt us, even the ones we're not proud of, teaches us something we need to know. The key is learning to extract the lesson without letting the experience define us.

Dancing taught me sales psychology, customer service, financial independence, and the power of personal branding. It also taught me some destructive patterns around self-worth, relationships, and money that I'd have to unlearn later.

The trick was keeping what served me and healing what hurt me.

That process would take years. But it started with recognizing that every choice I made—even the ones born from desperation—was preparing me for something bigger than I could see at the time.

BOSS TIP: Money That Comes Fast Often Leaves Faster

One of the biggest lessons from my dancing years is understanding the difference between quick money and sustainable wealth. Here's what I learned:

Quick Money Characteristics:

- Tied to your physical presence or time
- Requires you to constantly "perform" to maintain income
- Often comes with high emotional or psychological costs
- Usually has no growth potential—you hit a ceiling quickly
- Stops when you stop

Sustainable Wealth Characteristics:

- Can be built systematically over time
- Eventually works without your constant involvement (passive income)
- Grows exponentially rather than linearly

- Has multiple revenue streams
- Continues even when you're not actively working

The Bridge Strategy: If you're currently in a "quick money" situation—whether that's dancing, gig work, or any hustle that pays daily but doesn't build long-term—here's how to transition:

1. **Save a percentage of every dollar**: Even if it's just 10%, put something aside from every payment. Quick money can fund your transition to sustainable wealth if you're disciplined.

2. **Study the clients**: Pay attention to how your customers make their money. What businesses do they own? What skills do they have? Learn from the people who can afford to pay you.

3. **Develop transferable skills**: I learned sales, psychology, and customer service dancing. What skills are you developing that could transfer to legitimate business?

4. **Set an exit timeline**: Don't get comfortable in quick money. It's a means to an end, not the end itself. Give yourself a deadline to transition.

5. **Invest in your future self**: Use quick money to fund education, business startup costs, or skill development that will create longer-term opportunities.

Remember: there's no shame in doing what you need to do to survive. But survival is not the same as thriving. Always be working toward wealth that lasts longer than your ability to hustle for it.

CHAPTER 3

STREET ECONOMICS & SURVIVAL

D ancing was paying the bills, but it wasn't paying for the life I really wanted.

Don't get me wrong—the money was good for a teenager. But I was always that girl who could see ahead, who could visualize beyond my current circumstances. And when I looked at the women in their twenties and thirties still dancing, I saw my future if I didn't make a move. That scared me more than anything else.

I knew there was no longevity in that lifestyle. You're selling youth, beauty, and fantasy—all of which have expiration dates. I needed something bigger, something that could scale, something that didn't require me to be physically present to make money.

That's when I moved to Atlanta.

Moving to Atlanta from Jacksonville was like stepping into a different universe. For the first time in my life, I saw Black people—especially Black women—being successful in ways I'd never imagined. Not successful because they were attached to a successful man, but successful on their own terms, building their own empires.

In Jacksonville, the successful women I knew were the ones who had locked down a drug dealer or found a man with money. Your success was dependent on someone else's success. But in Atlanta? I saw women who were the dealers, the bosses, the ones calling the shots. They were driving their own cars, living in their own houses, making their own money.

I was immediately attracted to that energy, that possibility. And you know how it goes in Atlanta—whatever you put in motion there, good or bad, comes to pass. I put "getting money" in motion, and God delivered exactly what I asked for, though not how I expected.

I met this dude in traffic. Literally. I was driving down Roswell Road, and this man flagged me down from his car. Now, this was back in the day when that kind of thing wasn't as dangerous as it is now—or maybe we were all just more naive. Either way, I pulled over, we talked, and he introduced me to a whole different side of Atlanta.

This was before the recession hit, so money was flowing differently. Atlanta was booming, and if you knew how to position yourself, you could get a piece of that boom. He showed me the scamming world—credit card fraud, identity theft, document manipulation. The paper game.

I want to be clear about something: I'm not proud of this part of my story. I'm not glorifying criminal activity or suggesting anyone follow this path. What I am doing is being honest about the choices I made and the mindset that led to those choices, because understanding that mindset is crucial to understanding how I eventually redirected it toward legitimate success.

At that time, with my background and education level, traditional paths to wealth seemed impossible. I couldn't get approved for business loans with no credit and no collateral. I couldn't walk into corporate America with my work history. The systems that help people build legitimate wealth weren't designed for people like me.

So I learned the underground economy instead.

The credit card game was different from dancing. It required intelligence, strategy, and technology skills. You had to understand financial systems, human psychology, and risk management. You needed to be able to think three steps ahead, anticipate problems, and adapt quickly when things went wrong.

In many ways, it was excellent business training disguised as criminal activity.

I learned about profit margins—how much you could invest versus how much you could make back. I learned about inventory management—keeping the right documents, cards, and information on hand without holding too much risk. I learned about customer service—keeping the people you worked with happy and coming back for more.

Most importantly, I learned about scaling. Dancing was a one-to-one transaction—my time for their money. But scamming could be one-to-many. I could work one scheme and generate multiple revenue streams from it.

The money was incredible. More than I'd ever seen. We're talking about amounts that could change your life in a weekend if you played your cards right. I remember thinking, "This is what financial freedom feels like."

But I also learned about risk versus reward in the most visceral way possible. Because every dollar you make illegally comes with the threat of losing everything—your freedom, your future, your life.

I got caught up in more than just the credit card stuff. I was dating a drug dealer out in Marietta, so I was around that life too. I was carrying guns, moving in circles where violence was always a possibility. I was living multiple dangerous lives simultaneously, thinking I was smart enough to manage all the risks.

The truth is, I was addicted to the adrenaline as much as the money. There's something intoxicating about beating the system, about making more in a day than most people make in months, about living outside the rules that seem designed to keep people like you down.

But the game always comes to an end.

Mine ended on a morning when they kicked in my door. Federal agents, local police, the whole show. I was still in bed when they came, and suddenly my house was full of strangers with badges and guns, searching through everything I owned.

I knew they were going to find things. I had guns in there—never used them, but I had them. I had drugs—personal use, but still illegal. I had documents and evidence of the credit card schemes. I was caught red-handed in multiple felonies.

The funny thing is, even as it was happening, part of me couldn't believe it was real. You get so comfortable in illegal activity that you start to feel untouchable. You start to think you're smarter than the system. You forget that they've been playing this game longer than you've been alive.

But the most surreal part came later, in the interrogation room. The first detective wanted to talk about the credit card fraud. I knew enough to keep my mouth shut about that. But then the second detective came in and said, "I want to talk to you about the shooting at Doc's."

My blood went cold.

There had been an incident at this bar called Doc's in Cobb County. I'd gotten into it with a bartender who called me a racial slur. In my anger, I'd knocked everything off the bar counter. When two big white security guards physically threw me out—literally picked up all 130 pounds of me and threw me on the ground—I saw red.

I went to my car, grabbed my gun, and emptied the clip into the air until it was empty.

The moment I did it, I knew I'd fucked up. Not just made a mistake— fucked up in a way that could end my life. I packed up and ran to Jacksonville for a month, hoping it would all blow over. When I came back to Atlanta, I thought I was in the clear.

I wasn't.

Sitting in that interrogation room, facing charges that could add up to 40+ years in prison, I had a moment of absolute clarity about the path I'd been on. All the quick money, all the adrenaline, all the feeling of being above the system—it had led me to a concrete room where my life was in someone else's hands.

The detective who questioned me about the shooting could have charged me with two counts of aggravated assault. If he had, I'd still be in prison today. Instead, for reasons I'll never fully understand, he went back to the drawing board and charged me with "discharge of a weapon on the property of another without their permission."

I'd never heard of that charge before. Neither had my public defender. It was a misdemeanor instead of the felony that should have buried me.

That was favor. That was God. That was Jesus intervening in a way that saved my life and gave me a second chance I didn't deserve but desperately needed.

But before I understood it as favor, I had to sit in county jail for eight months, not knowing what was going to happen to me. Eight months to think about every choice that had led me to that cell. Eight months to decide who I wanted to be when I got out.

The illegal money had taught me real business skills—risk assessment, profit calculation, customer psychology, inventory management, team building. But it had also taught me that quick money without legitimate foundations is just borrowed time.

Sitting in that cell, I made myself a promise: if I got out, I would take everything I'd learned in the streets and apply it to legitimate business. I would use my hustle for legal enterprises. I would build wealth that couldn't be taken away by a search warrant.

I didn't know how yet. I just knew that the same intelligence, drive, and strategic thinking that had made me successful in illegal activities could make me successful in legal ones if I could just figure out how to channel it properly.

The streets had given me an MBA in survival economics. Prison was about to give me a PhD in perseverance and planning.

Everything I thought I knew about money, power, and success was about to be tested in ways I never imagined.

BLUEPRINT LESSON: Legitimate Hustle vs. Illegal Hustle: The Real ROI

The biggest lie about illegal money is that it's easier than legitimate money. Here's the truth about the real return on investment:

Illegal Money:

- Potential for quick, large returns
- Requires constant vigilance and stress management
- No legal protection for your investments or disputes
- Can't be reported on taxes or used for legitimate credit building
- Always carries the risk of losing everything (including freedom)
- No legitimate business credit or networks built
- Skills developed can't be listed on resumes or used for references

Legitimate Money:

- Slower initial growth but compound returns over time

- Legal protection for your business and investments
- Can be used to build credit, secure loans, and create generational wealth
- Skills and network building that accelerate future opportunities
- Reputation and credibility that open doors
- Peace of mind and sustainability

The Hidden Costs of Street Money:

1. **Stress Tax**: Illegal money comes with constant anxiety, paranoia, and sleep loss that affects your health and decision-making
2. **Relationship Tax**: You can't truly share your life with people who don't know how you really make money
3. **Time Tax**: Prison sentences don't just cost you freedom—they cost you years of wealth building when compound interest matters most
4. **Opportunity Tax**: Time spent on illegal activities is time not spent building legitimate skills and networks

Transferring Street Skills to Legal Success:

- Risk assessment → Business planning and investment strategy
- Customer psychology → Sales and marketing
- Team management → Leadership and delegation
- Profit calculation → Financial management and analysis
- Adaptation under pressure → Entrepreneurial problem-solving

If you're currently making money through questionable means, your goal should be to bridge into legitimate business as quickly as possible. The same skills that make you successful in the streets can make you wildly successful in business—but only if you redirect them before the streets redirect your life for you.

The smartest hustlers eventually become entrepreneurs. The question is whether you'll make that transition by choice or by force.

PART II:
THE FALL & THE
FOUNDATION

CHAPTER 4

THE DAY EVERYTHING CHANGED

The sound of your front door being kicked in at 6 AM is something you never forget.

BOOM. CRASH. Then voices—lots of them—shouting commands, identifying themselves as federal agents and local police. I went from deep sleep to wide awake terror in about two seconds, my heart hammering so hard I thought it might stop.

I knew immediately what this was about. When you're living multiple illegal lives, there's always a part of you waiting for this moment, even when you think you're being careful, even when you think you're smarter than the system.

But knowing it might happen and experiencing it are two completely different things.

Suddenly my bedroom—my sanctuary, my private space—was full of strangers with badges and guns. They were searching through everything: my dresser drawers, my closet, under my mattress, through my personal belongings like they owned them. Like I was already guilty and they were just collecting evidence to prove what they already knew.

I wasn't thinking clearly. How could I? I'd gone from dreams to nightmare in seconds. But even in my panic, I knew they were going to find things. The gun under my bed. The cocaine I used recreationally. The documents and credit cards from my schemes. I was caught red-handed in multiple felonies, and there was no talking my way out of it.

They cuffed me, read me my rights, and took me to Smyrna jail first. The whole ride there, I kept thinking this had to be some kind of mistake, some kind of bad dream I'd wake up from. Even though I knew what I'd been doing, even though I knew this day might come, part of me had convinced myself I was too smart to get caught.

The first reality check came in the booking process. The fingerprints, the photos, the paperwork—all of it designed to strip away your identity and reduce you to a number, a case file, a problem for the system to process. They don't see you as a person with a story, with reasons, with potential. You're just another criminal who got caught.

The second reality check came in that first interrogation room.

Detective number one wanted to talk about the credit card fraud. I wasn't stupid enough to start confessing to anything, so I kept my mouth shut. Take me back to my cell, I'll wait for a lawyer, whatever. I thought this was going to be straightforward—difficult, but straightforward.

Then detective number two walked in.

"I want to talk to you about the shooting at Doc's."

My blood went cold. How did they know about Doc's? That incident had happened months ago. I'd run to Jacksonville immediately after, stayed there for a month, and when I came back to Atlanta, nothing happened.

No calls, no visits, no follow-up. I thought it was over, forgotten, swept under the rug of too many other crimes for them to worry about.

I was wrong.

"You can talk to me about it now," he said, "or I can charge you with two counts of aggravated assault right now."

Aggravated assault. Two counts. I knew enough about the legal system to know that meant serious time—20 years to life serious. The kind of sentence that would end my story before it really began.

But something told me to talk. Maybe it was fear, maybe it was the Holy Spirit, maybe it was just survival instinct. But I felt like honesty was my only option in that moment.

So I told him everything.

I told him about going to Doc's that night, about being young and drunk and high. I told him about the argument with the bartender, how he called me a racial slur that sent me into a rage. I told him about knocking everything off the bar counter, about the two big white security guards who picked up all 130 pounds of me and threw me on the ground like a rag doll.

I told him about seeing red, about going to my car and grabbing my gun, about emptying the entire clip until there were no bullets left.

And I told him about the moment afterward when I knew—absolutely knew—that I had fucked up in a way that could end my life.

I was crying while I told this story. Not because I was trying to manipulate him, but because reliving that night forced me to confront how close I'd come to throwing away everything. How a few seconds of anger and a loaded gun had nearly cost me my entire future.

He listened to all of it. Then he said, "Let me see what I'm going to charge you with," and left me alone in that room.

I sat there for what felt like hours, but was probably minutes, thinking about everything that had led to this moment. All the choices, all the shortcuts, all the times I'd chosen the fast money over the safe money, the street respect over legitimate respect, the quick fix over the long-term solution.

This was where it had gotten me. Twenty-three years old, facing decades in prison, my whole life about to be decided by a man I'd just met.

When they moved me from Smyrna to the main jail in Marietta, I thought I'd be facing charges for both the shooting and the fraud. Multiple felonies, multiple cases, multiple ways for the system to bury me.

But something strange happened. When I got to Marietta, they only had the identity fraud charges on my paperwork. No shooting charges. No weapons charges. Nothing about Doc's.

I kept waiting for the other shoe to drop. For weeks, I'd wake up expecting them to call my name with additional charges. I even asked the guards about it—where were the other charges? There had to be other charges.

But there weren't.

A month later, they finally called my name with a green form—which meant misdemeanor charges. I was confused because how was a shooting incident a misdemeanor? How was "discharge of a weapon on the property of another without their permission" even a real charge?

I'd never heard of that charge before. My public defender had never heard of it. It was like the detective had gone back to the law books and found the most obscure, least serious charge he could apply to what I'd done.

If he had hit me with those aggravated assault charges, I'd still be in prison today. Twenty-two years to life would have meant I'd be lucky to get out before I was 45. My daughter would have grown up without me. This book would never exist. Everything I've built since then would just be dreams I had in a cell.

But instead, he chose mercy. He chose to see something in me that was worth saving, even though I couldn't see it in myself at the time.

The final plea deal was seven years, with one year to serve and six years of probation. Since I'd already been in county jail for eight months, I only had to do four more months in actual prison. Four months that would change my life forever.

But first, I had to face the reality of what I'd done. Not just the legal consequences, but the spiritual and emotional consequences. I had to sit with the fact that my choices had hurt people—the businesses I'd defrauded, the customers whose identities I'd stolen, the community I'd put at risk with my reckless behavior.

I had to acknowledge that I'd been living like someone with nothing to lose, when the truth was I had everything to lose. My freedom, my future, my ability to be present for the people I loved.

Most importantly, I had to confront the fact that all my illegal success had been an illusion. The money, the lifestyle, the feeling of beating the system—none of it was real if it could all disappear with one bad decision and a search warrant.

Sitting in that cell, waiting to be sentenced, I made myself a promise: if I got out of this situation, I would never again build my life on something that could be taken away by badges and handcuffs. I would take everything I'd learned about business, psychology, and strategy and apply it to legitimate enterprises.

I would transform my hustle, not abandon it.

I didn't know how yet. I just knew that the same intelligence and drive that had made me successful in the streets could make me successful in business if I could figure out how to channel it legally.

The day they sentenced me was the day my real education began. Not the kind you get in classrooms, but the kind you get when you're forced to rebuild yourself from nothing, with nothing but time, determination, and the painful clarity that comes from losing everything you thought mattered.

Prison was about to teach me lessons no business school could offer. About resilience, about planning, about the power of visualization and faith. About what you're truly made of when everything familiar is stripped away.

That sentencing day was the end of one version of my story. But it was also the beginning of the version that would lead to everything I am today.

Sometimes you have to lose everything to discover what you're actually capable of building.

BOSS TIP: When Everything Crumbles, That's Your Foundation

The moment when your world falls apart isn't the end of your story—it's often the beginning of your real story. Here's what I learned about turning rock bottom into bedrock:

Recognize the Gift in the Crisis:

- Crisis forces clarity. When everything is on the line, you stop lying to yourself about what matters
- Rock bottom becomes a solid foundation—you can't sink any lower, so the only direction is up
- Losing everything external forces you to develop internal resources you didn't know you had

Take Inventory Without Self-Pity:

1. **Skills Assessment**: What abilities did you develop even in your worst choices? I learned sales, psychology, and risk assessment through illegal activities—all transferable to business
2. **Network Evaluation**: Who stayed when things got bad? Those are your real supporters

3. **Character Audit**: What patterns got you here? What mindsets need to change?

Use Forced Stillness Strategically: Whether you're in actual prison or just in a life situation where you can't move forward immediately:

- Plan obsessively for your comeback
- Study everything you can get your hands on
- Visualize your future success in detail
- Write down specific goals and timelines

Transform Your Pain into Power:

- Your worst experiences become your greatest credibility in helping others
- Your mistakes become case studies for better decision-making
- Your recovery becomes proof that transformation is possible

Never Waste a Good Crisis: Every breakdown contains the seeds of a breakthrough if you're willing to:

- Take full responsibility without making excuses
- Learn the lessons completely so you don't have to repeat them
- Use the experience as fuel for your next level

The favor that saved me in that courtroom wasn't random—it was preparation meeting opportunity. I had to be ready to receive the mercy I was given and do something meaningful with it.

When your world crumbles, don't just survive it. Use it as raw material to build something stronger than what you had before.

CHAPTER 5

PRISON PRAYERS & PROMISES

P rison is designed to break you.

The concrete walls, the metal bars, the constant noise, the lack of privacy, the dehumanizing routine—everything about it is meant to strip away your sense of self until you're nothing but a number, a problem, a cautionary tale.

But here's what they don't tell you: sometimes breaking is exactly what you need to rebuild yourself stronger.

I spent my 24th birthday in prison. Twenty-four years old, sitting in a cell, thinking about how different my life looked from what I'd imagined at that age. I thought I'd be successful by then—and in some twisted way, I had been. I'd made more money than most people my age. I'd lived independently, called my own shots, answered to nobody.

But all of that success had been built on sand. One arrest, and it all disappeared like it never existed.

The first thing prison teaches you is that you have nothing but time. Time to think. Time to regret. Time to plan. Time to face everything you've been running from.

When you're on the streets, moving fast, chasing money, handling business, you don't have time for reflection. You're always reacting, always moving, always dealing with the next crisis or opportunity. But in prison, all that external noise stops. It's just you and your thoughts, 24 hours a day, for months or years.

That forced stillness was the beginning of everything for me.

I went through phases during my time inside. First was my "super saved" phase, where I dove headfirst into religion because I was scared and desperate and needed something bigger than myself to hold onto. I was praying constantly, reading the Bible, attending every service they offered. I wasn't just finding God—I was clinging to Him like a life raft.

Then I went through my "little boy" phase—don't ask me to explain that one. Prison does things to your mind when you're young and trying to figure out who you are. You experiment with different versions of yourself, different ways of surviving.

After that came my "thug out" phase, where I convinced myself I was harder than I actually was, that prison was making me stronger and more dangerous instead of more wise.

But eventually, I settled into what I call my planning phase. And that's where the real transformation began.

I started writing. Everything. My thoughts, my goals, my dreams, my plans for when I got out. I had this envelope full of papers that I filled with visions for my future. Some of it was fantasy—I thought I was going to be a rapper when I got out. I was writing songs, convinced I was going to go platinum.

But mixed in with the unrealistic dreams were some very specific, very detailed plans. I wrote about getting married. I wrote about going to college. I wrote about being successful in business. I wrote about having kids and breaking generational curses.

I didn't know it at the time, but I was doing advanced visualization work. I was writing the vision and making it plain, just like the Bible verse says. I was creating a blueprint for my future self, even though I called it daydreaming.

The crazy part is, when I finally found those papers years later—when I was packing to move from Atlanta to Hawaii after getting married—almost everything on those lists had come to pass. Not the rapper part, obviously. God had different plans for my talents. But the marriage, the success, the family, the business ownership—all of it had manifested exactly as I'd written it.

That's when I truly understood the power of writing down your goals. It's not just planning—it's programming your subconscious mind to recognize opportunities and make decisions that align with your vision.

Prison also taught me about people in ways I'd never experienced before. In county jail, you're dealing with chaos—people coming and going, fights breaking out, everyone stressed about their cases. But in actual prison, you're dealing with people who live there. That's their home, their world, their reality.

Some of them were exactly where they belonged. They were danger-ous, predatory, completely disconnected from any sense of humanity or redemption. Being around them reminded me that choices have conse-quences, and some consequences are permanent.

But others—and this broke my heart—were sweet women who'd made one terrible decision in a moment of desperation or rage. Women who'd killed abusive husbands. Women who'd gotten caught up in their boy-friend's crimes. Women who were serving life sentences for mistakes that took seconds to make but would cost them decades to pay for.

Meeting these women was my first real introduction to the concept of grace versus consequences. Some people get second chances, and some people don't. Some people's mistakes are forgiven, and some people's mistakes become their entire identity. I was one of the lucky ones—I got grace. But sitting next to women who didn't, who would never come home, who would die in that place—that humbled me in ways nothing else could.

It also scared the hell out of me. That could have been me. Should have been me, really, based on the charges I was facing. The only thing stand-ing between me and a life sentence was favor I didn't deserve.

That realization made me take my second chance seriously in a way I might not have otherwise.

Prison also taught me about loyalty—or the lack thereof. When you're locked up, you find out real quick who actually cares about you versus who was just around for the benefits. People who claimed to love me dis-appeared the moment I couldn't do anything for them. Folks I'd looked out for, helped financially, supported through their own drama—gone.

The only person who held me down consistently was my mother. The same woman I'd run away from, the same woman I'd been beefing with before I got locked up, the same woman whose communication style had driven me crazy—she was the only one putting money on my phone, money on my books, showing up for visits.

That experience completely transformed our relationship. I fell in love with my mother while I was in prison because she proved that blood is thicker than everything else when it really matters. All our fights, all our disagreements, all the ways we'd hurt each other—none of that mattered when I needed her most.

She was there. Period.

That taught me about conflict resolution in a way no therapy could have. It showed me that you can have love and loyalty even with people who trigger you, even with people who don't always handle you the way you want to be handled. My mother wasn't perfect, but she was consistent when consistency mattered most.

From that point forward, I decided that's how I would handle our relationship. We might disagree, we might argue, but we were going to love each other through it and move forward together. No more holding grudges. No more letting past hurts poison present relationships.

The spiritual awakening I experienced in prison wasn't just about finding God—it was about finding myself. For the first time in my life, I had to sit with who I really was underneath all the performance, all the survival mechanisms, all the roles I'd been playing.

I wasn't the tough girl from the streets. I wasn't the independent woman who didn't need anybody. I wasn't the smart criminal who could out-smart the system. All of those identities had been stripped away, and what was left was just Barbie—young, scared, hurt, but still alive and still capable of change.

I started to understand that everything I'd been through—the abuse, the running away, the dancing, the scamming—had been my attempt to gain control over a life that had felt out of control since I was nine years old. I'd been trying to protect myself, provide for myself, and prove my worth through external achievements and acquisitions.

But sitting in that cell, with nothing and no one, I realized that real power comes from internal work. Real security comes from knowing who you are regardless of what you have. Real worth comes from understanding your purpose beyond just survival.

I started to pray differently. Instead of just asking God to get me out of trouble, I started asking Him to show me what He wanted me to do with my life. Instead of just reading the Bible for comfort, I started studying it for wisdom and direction.

I began to understand that my experiences—even the painful ones, even the shameful ones—could be used to help other people. That my story of falling down could become a story of getting back up. That my mistakes could become lessons for someone else who was heading down the same path.

That's when I first felt called to something bigger than just personal success. I felt called to use whatever platform I was given to bring other people with me. To become living proof that your past doesn't have to determine your future.

I made God a promise while I was locked up: if He got me out and gave me another chance, I would use my life to serve others. I would use my story to help people avoid the mistakes I'd made. I would use whatever success I achieved to create opportunities for people who looked like me, came from where I came from, and had been through what I'd been through.

That promise became the foundation of everything I've built since then.

When I finally got out after serving my time, I had that envelope full of papers with all my goals and dreams written down. But more importantly, I had a new understanding of who I was and what I was capable of.

I wasn't just a survivor anymore. I was a woman with a purpose, a plan, and the spiritual backing to make it all happen.

Prison was supposed to be my punishment. Instead, it became my preparation for everything God had planned for my life.

BLUEPRINT LESSON: Write the Vision, Make it Plain

The most powerful tool I discovered in prison wasn't available in the library or the commissary—it was a pen and paper. Here's how to harness the life-changing power of writing down your vision:

Why Writing Goals Works:

- **Clarity**: Writing forces you to be specific about what you actually want versus what sounds good

- **Commitment**: There's something psychological about putting pen to paper that makes goals feel more real
- **Programming**: Your subconscious mind starts working on solutions when you clearly define problems and objectives
- **Accountability**: Written goals become a contract with yourself

The Prison Method of Visualization:

1. **Write in Detail**: Don't just write "I want to be successful." Write "I will own a six-figure business teaching other women financial literacy by age 30."
2. **Include Emotions**: How will you feel when you achieve this goal? What will your daily life look like? Who will you be helping?
3. **Set Timelines**: Give yourself deadlines. Without timelines, goals are just wishes.
4. **Review Regularly**: I read my goals every day in prison. Repetition programs your mind for success.
5. **Update as You Grow**: Your vision should evolve as you do. What you want at 20 might be different from what you want at 30.

The Power of Forced Stillness: Whether you're in prison, recovery, unemployment, or any other situation that forces you to slow down:

- Use the time to plan instead of just waiting
- Study everything you can about your next move
- Build the internal foundation that external success requires
- Connect with your purpose beyond just making money

From Visualization to Manifestation: Writing goals is just the first step. To turn vision into reality:

- Take daily actions aligned with your written goals
- Speak your vision into existence through positive self-talk
- Surround yourself with people who support your transformation
- Stay faithful to the process even when progress feels slow

The goals I wrote in that prison cell became the blueprint for my entire life. That envelope of papers was worth more than any business degree because it contained my authentic vision for my future.

Your circumstances don't determine your destiny—your vision does. Start writing yours today.

PART III:
THE REBUILD - FINDING
LEGITIMATE LANES

CHAPTER 6

HAWAII HAPPENINGS
- THE UNEXPECTED PIVOT

When I got out of prison in 2009, I had big plans. I was going to join the Army, get my life together through military structure, and build a legitimate career. I had it all mapped out—the same strategic thinking that had gotten me in trouble was now going to get me out of it.

Then God laughed at my plans.

The year I got out, 2010, they changed the military policy. Felons could no longer enlist. My carefully constructed plan A disappeared overnight, leaving me scrambling for a plan B I hadn't prepared for.

I should have been devastated. Instead, I was about to learn one of the most important lessons of my entrepreneurial journey: sometimes the doors that close are blessings in disguise, redirecting you toward opportunities you never would have considered.

My best friend Lita—who I call my CEO because she's been my business partner in so many ventures—had been telling me for years to come visit her in Hawaii. She was military, stationed there, and she kept saying, "You need to come to Hawaii. You'll love it here."

Hawaii? I'm from Jacksonville, Florida. My idea of exotic was Atlanta. Hawaii seemed like a vacation destination for rich people, not a place where someone like me could build a life.

But when my Army plans fell through, Lita's invitation started sounding different. What was I holding onto in Atlanta anyway? What was keeping me tied to a place where I had more bad memories than good opportunities?

For my 27th birthday, Lita flew me and my daughter out to Hawaii. Just a visit, she said. Just come see what it's like.

The trip almost didn't happen. We were flying on buddy passes, which meant we kept getting bumped from flights when paying customers needed the seats. For two days, we sat in the airport, watching flight after flight take off without us. I was ready to give up and go to Vegas instead—at least I knew I could get there and make some quick money dancing.

But something told me to keep trying. I remember standing outside the airport, smoking a cigarette and crying because I was so frustrated, and I said out loud: "There must be a life changing blessing waiting for me in Hawaii, because something is really trying to stop me from getting there."

That was prophetic words, though I didn't know it at the time.

Finally, the airline agent—who had to be an angel in disguise—told us we could get there if we separated. My daughter and I would fly into Kauai, and Lita would fly into Kona on the Big Island. We'd all connect to Oahu from our different islands. The idea of flying to islands I'd never been to with my 9-year-old daughter, to meet up with someone I hadn't seen in person for years, should have terrified me.

Instead, it felt like a trust exercise with God. Like He was saying, "Are you willing to do something you've never done to get something you've never had?"

So we did it. We took that leap of faith, flew to Kauai with my baby girl, and met up with Lita in Oahu. Everything worked out perfectly, like it was orchestrated by something bigger than our planning.

The first few days in Hawaii were everything Lita had promised. Beautiful beaches, perfect weather, a pace of life that felt completely different from anywhere I'd ever lived. But the real life change came through a series of connections that seemed too perfectly timed to be coincidental.

Lita had posted on Facebook that she was home, and her childhood friend Chris—who she'd gone to high school with—saw the post and offered to pick us up from the airport. Chris had been carrying a torch for Lita since high school, but she'd never seen him as more than a friend.

We all started hanging out, and one night we were drinking and joking about military marriages—you know, those quick marriages that military people sometimes do for the benefits. The housing allowance, the increased pay, the base privileges. We were adding up the numbers like a business proposal.

"If we got married," Chris said to Lita, "we'd be pulling in about three grand a month."

"If I got married too," I joked, "that's six grand a month total."

It started as a joke. But jokes have a way of becoming reality when you're not careful with your words.

Chris got serious first. He told me he'd always been in love with Lita, that he'd dreamed of marrying her since high school. I could see the genuine emotion in his eyes, so I encouraged him. "You should ask her," I said. "Life's short. What's the worst that could happen?"

He asked her the next day. She said yes. They went downtown to the courthouse and got married that afternoon.

And I'm following behind them in my rental car, playing Jay-Z's "On the Run Part II," talking to myself about how love isn't real and fairy tales don't exist. I was in my cynic era, convinced that what I was witnessing was just a business transaction dressed up as romance.

But Chris had a friend. His name was Jaren, and when Chris introduced us that night, I saw this tall, dark-skinned man and thought, "Okay, that's him."

I ran the marriage proposal by Jaren like a business pitch. He was living in the barracks, wanting to get out. I couldn't go to college and dance at the same time—I'd tried that before and failed. This could be a win-win situation for both of us.

He had to go out to sea for a week before he could give me an answer. When he came back, we spent a week getting to know each other. At the end of that week, he said, "If we're going to do this, we're going to do it for real. You're not going to be dancing anymore."

I hadn't expected that. The marriage was supposed to be a business arrangement, not a real relationship with real rules and expectations.

"You need to move to Hawaii," he continued. "We need to actually be married if we're going to be married."

This man was six years younger than me, but he had an old soul and clear boundaries. He wasn't playing games or pretending this was just about money. If we were going to do this, we were going to commit to it fully.

So I did something completely out of character for me: I said yes to uncertainty. I agreed to move across the Pacific Ocean to marry a man I'd known for seven days, to start a life in a place I'd visited for two weeks.

We got married at a Starbucks in Aiea, Hawaii. Not the most romantic setting, but it felt right for who we were and how we'd met. No pretense, no fairy tale expectations, just two people making a practical decision that we hoped might become something more.

When I moved to Hawaii permanently, I hated it at first. Hawaii is beautiful if you're on vacation or if you're rich enough to live near the beaches. But if you're a regular person trying to make a living, it can feel like a third world country. Everything costs more because it has to be shipped over water. A gallon of milk was $10. Gas was outrageous. The luxury tax on everything made even basic necessities feel like splurges.

I was depressed for months. I'd left everything familiar—my family, my friends, my ways of making money—to start over in a place where I knew nobody and had no idea how to build a life.

But depression has a way of forcing innovation when you can't afford to stay stuck.

I had to figure out how to make money legally, and I had to do it fast. Dancing wasn't an option anymore—my husband had made that clear, and honestly, I was ready to try something different anyway.

That's when my friend Lita suggested I post my hair work on a Facebook page called "Hawaii Weaves." I'd always done hair—my own, my friends', whoever needed it—but I'd never thought of it as a real business.

"Just post your work," she said. "See what happens."

I was reluctant. What work? I was just doing hair in my house, learning as I went, trying to make myself and my friends look cute.

But Lita grabbed my phone and posted for me. "If she won't do it, I will," she said, and uploaded photos of some hair I'd done.

Within hours, my phone was blowing up. Women all over the island wanting appointments, asking about prices, booking sessions.

I had stumbled into my first legitimate business without even realizing it.

I started simple: sew-ins for $100, and I'd come to you. This was before the wig wave really took off, when most women were still doing traditional weaves and protective styles. I was mobile, affordable, and available— three things that were in short supply on an island where everything was expensive and hard to get.

The appointments started coming faster than I could handle them. Women who couldn't afford $200+ for hair in Honolulu were thrilled to find someone charging Atlanta prices in Hawaii. I was building a client base by accident, just by being reasonable and reliable.

But the real breakthrough came when I started selling hair, not just styling it.

In Hawaii, because of the luxury tax and shipping costs, hair bundles that cost $50 in Atlanta were selling for $200+ in beauty supply stores. And most of the time, you had to order them and wait—nobody kept good inventory on hand.

I remembered the first rule of drug dealing: keep product on deck. If someone wants something and you have it while your competition doesn't, you win.

So I started ordering hair directly from China and keeping inventory in my house. When women called for appointments, I could not only do their hair—I could sell them the hair too, at Atlanta prices in Hawaii— prices lower than the beauty supply stores but higher than what I paid for the hair directly.

I was accidentally creating a business model that would eventually make me millions: identify an underserved market, provide a superior product at a competitive price, and keep inventory available when customers want it.

The money started coming in faster than I'd ever experienced legitimately. Some days I was making $1,000+, meeting clients in Walmart parking lots and Starbucks, selling hair out of my trunk like I used to sell everything else.

I remember one day driving away from a sale, checking my rearview mirror out of habit, and realizing I was looking for police. Then it hit me: I wasn't doing anything illegal. I was running a legitimate business, making legal money, building something that couldn't be taken away by a search warrant.

That realization was freedom in a way I'd never experienced.

I called my mother, excited, and told her about my breakthrough moment. She laughed so hard because it was such a perfect metaphor for my transition from street life to business life. Same hustle, same sales skills, same customer service—just legal now.

Within months, I was making more money with hair than I'd ever made dancing, and I was building something sustainable instead of just trading time for money.

But the real magic happened when I decided to level up from mobile services to an actual location.

I'll never forget walking through the PX (the military shopping center) on base during my first visit to Hawaii and pointing at an empty kiosk. "I'm going to put a business right there," I'd said, not knowing what business, not having any real plan, just knowing that's where I belonged.

A year later, a kiosk became available—not the exact one I'd pointed at, but the one right behind it. Close enough for me to know this was meant to be. I signed the lease, quit my corporate job (yes, I'd gotten a legitimate job too, but that's another story), and opened Barbie's Star Status Hair.

My mother thought I'd lost my mind. "You're going to quit a good job to sell hair?" she asked. Every family member in Jacksonville called to tell me I was making a mistake.

But I knew I had to make the jump. God had been preparing me for this moment through every experience I'd had—the street sales, the customer psychology, the inventory management, the ability to read people and markets.

Opening day was magical. I'd put a commercial on the radio, had the radio station come to my grand opening, and sold every piece of hair I had. Fifteen thousand dollars in one day—more money than I'd ever made legally in such a short time.

But it wasn't just about the money. It was about proving to myself that I could build something legitimate, something that would last, something I could be proud of.

Hawaii had given me something I didn't even know I needed: the space and opportunity to discover who I could become when I wasn't just surviving, but actually building.

That kiosk was the foundation of everything that came after. It was where I learned the fundamentals of legitimate business—customer service, inventory management, marketing, branding. It was where I discovered I had a gift for entrepreneurship that went far beyond just making quick money.

Most importantly, it was where I started to see myself differently. Not as someone who'd made mistakes, but as someone who was learning from those mistakes to build something bigger.

Later, when we moved to Virginia, I would rebrand to Billionaires Hair as my vision expanded and my confidence grew.

Hawaii was supposed to be just a visit. Instead, it became the place where I found my legitimate hustle, and the first real proof that my business vision could work in the real world.

Sometimes the best opportunities come disguised as the biggest risks. You just have to be brave enough to take them.

BOSS TIP: Sometimes Your Breakthrough Comes Through Unexpected Doors

The military rejection that felt like a setback was actually a setup for something better. Here's how to recognize and navigate unexpected opportunities:

Signs You're Being Redirected (Not Rejected):

- Doors keep closing despite your best efforts
- You feel pulled toward something that doesn't make logical sense
- Opportunities arise that you never would have pursued otherwise
- People keep suggesting the same alternative path

How to Navigate Uncertain Opportunities:

1. **Trust Your Gut Over Your Logic**: Sometimes the best opportunities look crazy on paper but feel right in your spirit
2. **Do Your Research, But Don't Over-Research**: I didn't know everything about Hawaii, but I knew enough to take the leap
3. **Start Small, Think Big**: I didn't move to Hawaii to build a hair empire—I moved for marriage benefits. The business opportunity revealed itself later

4. **Leverage Your Existing Skills**: Everything I'd learned in the streets—sales, customer psychology, inventory management—translated directly to legitimate business

5. **Keep Your Overhead Low Initially**: I started mobile, working out of my house, before investing in a physical location

The Power of Geographic Arbitrage: Moving to Hawaii taught me about market gaps:

- Products that are common in one place might be scarce in another
- Pricing that seems normal in one market might be premium in another
- Skills that are saturated in one area might be in high demand elsewhere

When to Make the Jump:

- You've done your due diligence but still feel called to move
- You have enough savings to survive the transition period
- The opportunity aligns with your larger vision, even if the path is unclear
- You're more excited than scared (or at least equally both)

Trust the Process: Not every closed door is a rejection—sometimes it's protection from settling for less than what's meant for you. The Army rejection forced me to discover entrepreneurship. What feels like your biggest disappointment might be redirecting you toward your biggest opportunity.

Pay attention to patterns. When the same type of opportunity or suggestion keeps appearing in your life, that's usually God trying to tell you something. Your breakthrough might be waiting behind the door you're most hesitant to open.

CHAPTER 7

BARBIE'S STAR STATUS HAIR - BUILDING A BRAND FROM SCRATCH

That kiosk in the PX became my first real classroom in legitimate business—and let me tell you, the lessons came fast and hard.

I thought I knew about business because I'd made money illegally. I thought sales was just about convincing people to buy something they might not need. I thought success was just about making more money than you spent.

I was wrong about almost everything.

Running a legitimate business taught me that there's a massive difference between hustling and building. Hustling is about the quick win, the immediate profit, the next transaction. Building is about creating something that lasts, something that grows, something that works even when you're not physically present.

The kiosk forced me to learn building.

My first lesson came on day one when I realized I couldn't just wing it anymore. When you're selling credit cards or dancing, if you mess up, you find new customers. But when you have a physical location, when people know where to find you, when your reputation travels through military wives who all talk to each other—you better deliver exactly what you promise, every single time.

I had to learn about inventory management the hard way. I'd order too much of one texture and run out of another. I'd have beautiful 22-inch bundles but no 14-inch. I'd stock every color except the one three customers wanted that week.

But with each mistake, I got smarter. I started tracking what sold fastest, what customers asked for most, what trends were starting versus ending. I turned my kiosk into a laboratory for understanding consumer behavior.

The radio commercial was my first real lesson in marketing. I'd saved up enough money to buy a spot on the local station, and I thought I was so smart putting my business on the radio like the big companies.

The day it aired, my phone started ringing off the hook. But here's what I wasn't prepared for: having the demand but not the supply. I sold out completely—which sounds like a good problem to have until you realize that turning customers away because you don't have inventory is lost money you can never get back.

That experience taught me about scaling and preparation. You don't just need a good product and good marketing—you need the infrastructure to handle success when it comes.

The grand opening day was pure magic, though. $15,000 in one day, selling hair bundles and wigs to military wives who'd been paying mainland prices for island convenience. I remember standing in that kiosk at the end of the day, counting money that I'd made completely legally, from a business I'd built from scratch, serving customers who were genuinely happy with what they'd purchased.

That feeling was better than any drug, any adrenaline rush, any quick money I'd ever made illegally. This was mine. This was legitimate. This was something I could build on.

But then came the lesson that would define my entire approach to business from that point forward: the quarter-million-dollar disaster.

By the time I had my systems figured out in Hawaii, I was doing consistent six-figure revenue. I'd built a loyal customer base, figured out my inventory patterns, and established myself as the go-to person for quality hair on the island.

When we got orders to move to Virginia—military life means you go where they send you—I thought I could replicate that success anywhere. I was wrong about that too.

Virginia was a completely different market. First, the cost of living was lower, so people had less disposable income to spend on premium hair. Second, there were more options, so I wasn't filling an underserved niche anymore. Third, I was starting from zero again—no customer base, no reputation, no word-of-mouth marketing.

But I was determined to make it work. So when the opportunity came to do a massive hair sale—$250,000 worth of orders in three days—I thought it was my breakthrough moment.

I was wrong. It was my breakdown moment.

I'd found a supplier who taught me everything about hair quality, about spotting good hair from bad hair, about what customers really wanted versus what they said they wanted. This supplier had been mentoring me, helping me understand the business beyond just buying and selling.

When the big sale opportunity came up, they offered to fulfill the entire order for $80,000. I wired the money—first mistake. Never, ever wire money for large transactions unless you have ironclad protections in place.

What arrived was not what I'd paid for. The supplier gave me good hair on top of the boxes and trash underneath. These wigs were terrible. Unusable. Embarrassing.

But I'd already taken orders from 1,500 customers. These were real people who'd paid real money expecting real quality. I couldn't ship out garbage with my name on it.

So I made the decision that nearly bankrupted me: I found another supplier and paid another $80,000 to fulfill the orders properly. Now I was $160,000 deep into a sale that was supposed to generate $70,000 in profit.

While I was waiting for the replacement inventory—which took three weeks—customers started getting impatient. Some started calling me a scammer. That word hit different coming from legitimate customers than it did from street associates. These were women who'd trusted me with their money for a legal purchase, and I was letting them down through no fault of my own.

The whole thing became a public disaster on social media. People were making videos about how Billionaire Barbie had scammed them, how I'd taken their money and disappeared, how I was just another fake entrepreneur who couldn't deliver.

It was the most humbling experience of my business life.

I could have disappeared. I could have filed bankruptcy. I could have quit the hair business and tried something else. Instead, I did something that saved my reputation and taught me the most valuable lesson about crisis management:

I told the truth.

I made a video explaining exactly what had happened. I showed the bad hair I'd received. I explained why there were delays. I showed proof of the replacement orders I'd placed. I took full responsibility for not having better safeguards in place, and I committed to making every customer whole, even if it cost me everything.

That transparency saved my business. Not immediately—my sales never quite recovered to that $250,000 level again. But it saved my credibility and taught me something invaluable about authentic communication with customers.

People will forgive mistakes if you're honest about them. They'll work with you through problems if you take responsibility and show them you're solving those problems. But they'll never forgive being lied to or feeling like you're trying to hide something from them.

The quarter-million-dollar disaster also taught me about scaling responsibly. Just because you can handle a certain level of business doesn't mean you're ready for 10 times that level. Growth has to be sustainable, manageable, and backed by systems that can handle the increased volume.

But most importantly, it taught me that failure isn't the end of your story—it's data for your next chapter.

After that experience, I completely changed how I approached business. I became obsessed with customer service, logistics, and clear communication. I built systems to prevent the problems that had caused the disaster. I developed backup suppliers and never again put all my eggs in one basket.

I also became religious about not overpromising. Better to under-promise and over-deliver than to create expectations you can't meet.

By the time COVID hit in 2020, I was ready for another pivot. The hair business had taught me everything I needed to know about running a legitimate enterprise. I understood profit margins, customer psychology, inventory management, marketing, and crisis management.

But COVID changed everything overnight. Supply chains were disrupted. Customers stopped spending on luxury items like hair. International shipping became unreliable. The foundation of my business model was crumbling.

Instead of panicking, I asked myself: What have I learned that doesn't depend on physical products?

The answer was everything. The customer service skills, the marketing knowledge, the sales psychology, the ability to build trust and maintain relationships—all of that was transferable to any business model.

So I pivoted to digital. I started teaching other women how to do what I'd learned to do. Instead of selling hair bundles, I started selling knowledge. Instead of managing inventory, I started managing information.

The hair business had been my MBA in entrepreneurship. Every mistake, every success, every customer interaction had taught me something about how business really works at a fundamental level.

When I eventually transitioned into taxes, credit repair, and business consulting, I wasn't starting from scratch. I was applying proven principles to new industries. The same systems that had made me successful in hair could make me successful in financial services.

But it all started with that kiosk in Hawaii. With learning to build instead of just hustle. With understanding that legitimate business is about creating value for other people, not just extracting money from them.

The hair business taught me that your first business probably won't be your last business, but it will be your most important business. Because it's where you learn the fundamentals that everything else builds on.

It's where you discover whether you're really an entrepreneur or just someone who wants to make quick money. It's where you learn to handle success and failure with equal grace. It's where you figure out what you're really made of when everything goes wrong.

Most importantly, it's where you learn that building something legitimate—something that serves people, something that lasts, something you can be proud of—is worth more than any amount of quick money you could ever make.

The quarter-million-dollar loss hurt financially, but it was worth every penny for the education it gave me. Those lessons became the foundation for everything I built afterward.

Your first business might not make you rich, but if you pay attention, it will make you ready for the business that does.

BLUEPRINT LESSON: Your First Business Will Teach You Everything

Every entrepreneur needs a "tuition business"—the one that costs you money but gives you an education worth more than any degree. Here's how to extract maximum value from your learning business:

Essential Systems to Build Early:

1. **Customer Communication**: Always over-communicate. Tell people what's happening before they have to ask
2. **Inventory Management**: Know what you have, what you need, and what you're running low on
3. **Financial Tracking**: Understand your real profit margins, not just your gross revenue
4. **Quality Control**: Your reputation is built one transaction at a time
5. **Crisis Management**: Plan for things to go wrong, because they will

The Transparency Advantage: When problems arise (and they will):

- Acknowledge them quickly and publicly
- Take full responsibility without making excuses

- Show exactly how you're fixing the situation
- Over-deliver on your solutions
- Use the experience to improve your systems

Scaling Lessons:

- Don't multiply your problems by growing too fast
- Build systems before you need them
- Test your capacity before taking on large orders
- Have backup suppliers/solutions for everything critical
- Know the difference between growth and sustainable growth

Why Product Businesses Are Great Teacher Businesses:

- Immediate feedback from customers
- Clear metrics (inventory, sales, profit margins)
- Forces you to learn operations, marketing, and customer service
- Teaches you about supply chains and logistics
- Shows you the real cost of doing business

Extracting Transferable Skills: Everything you learn in your first business applies to future businesses:

- Customer psychology is the same across industries
- Sales processes are fundamentally similar
- Marketing principles work for any product or service
- Crisis management skills transfer anywhere
- System building becomes easier with practice

When to Pivot vs. When to Push Through:

- Pivot when the market fundamentally changes (like COVID)
- Push through when the problems are operational (like bad suppliers)
- Pivot when you've extracted the key lessons
- Push through when you're just hitting normal growing pains

The Real ROI of Your First Business: Your first business is rarely your most profitable, but it's always your most educational. The goal isn't to make millions—it's to learn millions of dollars worth of business lessons that you can apply to bigger opportunities later.

Don't measure your first business just by its financial returns. Measure it by what it teaches you about yourself, about customers, about markets, and about what it really takes to build something that lasts.

Every mistake in your tuition business is a lesson you don't have to learn again in your empire business.

CHAPTER 8

FROM NOBODY TO SOMEBODY - THE CELEBRITY STYLIST ERA

After the quarter-million-dollar lesson in Virginia, I was ready for a change of scenery and a change of strategy. The hair business had taught me everything about operations, but I was starting to understand that there were levels to this game that I hadn't even seen yet.

That's when Hollywood called.

Well, not exactly called. More like I positioned myself where Hollywood could find me.

By 2017, I was back and forth between Virginia and Los Angeles, working on sets for shows like "Love & Hip Hop Hollywood," "Basketball Wives," and "Hip Hop Squares." The entertainment industry was hungry for skilled hair stylists who could work with Black women's hair, and I'd developed a technique that was about to change everything.

I called it "Real Scalp Illusion."

Before I explain what that is, you need to understand where the hair industry was at that time. Most women were still doing sew-ins, closures, and traditional weaves. Lace front wigs existed, but they were expensive, hard to install properly, and honestly, most of them looked fake.

I was obsessed with making wigs look like they were growing out of your scalp. Not just "oh, that's a nice wig" but "wait, is that her real hair?" I spent countless hours perfecting the technique—how to cut the lace, how to apply it, how to style it so the hairline looked completely natural.

When I started posting videos of my work on Instagram, showing the before-and-after transformations, people lost their minds. I was waking up to 1,000 to 2,000 new followers every day. The technique was so revolutionary that other stylists started trying to copy it, but they couldn't replicate the results.

That's when I learned one of the most important lessons about building a personal brand: your technique can be copied, but your skill level can't be duplicated overnight.

Working with celebrities taught me about a completely different level of business. These women weren't just buying hair—they were investing in their image, their brand, their ability to make money. When you're getting paid millions to be photographed, your hair isn't a luxury expense—it's a business expense.

The celebrity clients started bringing me massive exposure. When you do someone's hair and they post it to millions of followers, that's marketing you can't buy. When they bring you on set with them, when they recommend you to their friends, when they tag you in their posts—that's social proof at the highest level.

But more importantly, these women became real friends. They weren't just treating me like "the help"—they genuinely enjoyed my company, wanted to hang out, wanted to party together. They were bringing me into their circles, introducing me to their networks, treating me like family.

This taught me something crucial about business: people don't just buy your product or service—they buy you. If they like you as a person, if they trust you, if they enjoy being around you, they'll choose you over technically better competitors every time.

The celebrity connections also taught me about scaling influence. When you're good at what you do, and you're working with people who have platforms, your reputation grows exponentially instead of linearly. One satisfied celebrity client is worth a thousand regular customers in terms of exposure and credibility.

But the real game-changer wasn't just the celebrity connections—it was learning how to document and teach what I was doing.

I started filming myself working. Not just the final results, but the actual process. How I cut the lace. How I applied the adhesive. How I styled the hair to create that scalp illusion. How I made adjustments to fit different face shapes and hairlines.

These weren't just Instagram posts—they were masterclasses disguised as content.

Women were commenting things like "I've been trying to figure out how to do this for years" and "Can you teach this?" and "Do you have a class?"

That's when the lightbulb went off. I wasn't just a hair stylist—I was sitting on a goldmine of teachable skills that other stylists desperately wanted to learn.

So I started offering classes. First in person, traveling to different cities, teaching small groups of stylists the Real Scalp Illusion technique. The classes would sell out within hours of being announced.

I was charging $500-$1,000 per student, and I'd have 20-30 students per class. Do the math—I was making more in one weekend teaching than most stylists make in a month doing hair.

But the real revelation came when I realized I could scale this even further by going digital.

This was before online education was as mainstream as it is now. Most people were still thinking about teaching as something that happened in physical classrooms. But I saw the potential to teach thousands of people simultaneously through digital platforms.

When COVID hit in 2020 and everyone was on lockdown, I created my first online course, breaking down the Real Scalp Illusion technique into step-by-step modules. I priced it at $99, thinking that was reasonable for what I was teaching.

It sold like crazy. Hundreds of sales in the first week. I realized I was severely underpricing myself.

More importantly, I realized I'd found a business model that could scale infinitely without requiring my physical presence. I could create a course once and sell it thousands of times. I could teach people while I was sleeping, while I was on vacation, while I was working with other clients.

This was my first real taste of passive income, and it was intoxicating.

But the celebrity era also taught me some hard lessons about managing success and staying grounded.

The money was flowing. The followers were growing. The opportunities were expanding. It would have been easy to get caught up in the lifestyle, to start believing my own hype, to think that success was guaranteed forever.

Instead, I watched other people in the industry make those mistakes and learned from their failures instead of my own.

I saw stylists who got big heads and started treating regular clients poorly. I saw influencers who thought their 15 minutes of fame would last forever and didn't build sustainable businesses behind their popularity. I saw people who got comfortable and stopped innovating, only to watch younger, hungrier competitors pass them by.

Those observations taught me about the importance of staying humble, staying hungry, and always looking for the next level.

The celebrity era was also when I started really understanding the power of personal branding versus business branding. For years, I'd been building "Billionaires Hair" as a business brand. But what was really growing was my personal brand—Billionaire Barbie.

People weren't just buying from Billionaires Hair anymore. They were buying from me, specifically. They wanted to learn from me, work with me, be connected to me. My personality, my story, my approach to business—that was becoming more valuable than any specific product or service I offered.

This realization would become crucial later when I pivoted away from hair entirely. Because I'd built a personal brand, not just a product brand, I could take my audience with me into any industry I chose to enter.

The celebrity era lasted about three years, and during that time I went from being a local hair stylist in Virginia to being recognized as one of the top wig specialists in the country. I had celebrity clients, social media followers, and a waiting list for my services.

But I was also getting tired.

The travel was exhausting. The pressure to constantly create new content was overwhelming. The demands of celebrity clients—who expected 24/7 availability and perfect results every time—were burning me out.

More importantly, I was starting to see the limitations of being a service provider, even a high-end one. There were only so many hours in my day, only so many clients I could take, only so much I could charge before pricing myself out of the market.

I wanted to build something bigger than a service business. I wanted to create systems that worked without me. I wanted multiple revenue streams that could generate income whether I was actively working or not.

The celebrity era had given me credibility, connections, and capital. But most importantly, it had given me a platform and a personal brand that I could leverage into bigger opportunities.

I just didn't know what those opportunities would be yet.

What I did know was that the same principles that had made me successful in hair could be applied to any industry: find an underserved market, develop a superior technique, document your process, teach others to do what you do, and scale through digital platforms.

I also knew that whatever I did next needed to be bigger than just personal success. The platform I'd built came with responsibility—responsibility to help other women, to share knowledge, to create opportunities for people who looked like me and came from where I came from.

The celebrity era was coming to an end, but the empire era was just beginning.

BOSS TIP: Position Yourself Where Opportunity Lives

Success isn't just about what you know—it's about who knows what you know. Here's how to strategically position yourself for exponential growth:

The Proximity Principle: Your network determines your net worth, but your proximity determines your network. Position yourself physically and digitally where your ideal clients and collaborators spend their time.

For my celebrity clientele, that meant:

- Being in Los Angeles during pilot season
- Attending industry events and parties
- Working on sets where other stylists and artists gathered
- Building relationships with people who had access to the rooms I wanted to enter

Document Everything:

- Film your process, not just your results
- Share your techniques and knowledge openly
- Create content that provides real value, not just promotional material
- Let people see how the magic happens

The Teaching Multiplier: When you can do something well:

- One-to-one service = Linear income (limited by your time)
- One-to-many teaching = Exponential income (unlimited by your time)
- Digital courses = Passive income (works while you sleep)

Build Personal Brand Over Product Brand:

- People buy from people they know, like, and trust
- Your personality and story become your biggest differentiator
- Personal brands can pivot across industries; product brands cannot
- Authenticity beats perfection every time

Strategic Relationship Building:

- Serve before you ask
- Add value to every interaction
- Treat everyone with respect, regardless of their current status
- Remember that today's assistant might be tomorrow's executive

The Platform Responsibility: When your influence grows:

- Use it to elevate others
- Share knowledge freely
- Create opportunities for people who remind you of your former self
- Remember that your success is supposed to serve a purpose bigger than yourself

Scaling Beyond Service: Service businesses have income ceilings. To break through:

- Systematize your expertise into teachable frameworks
- Create products that work without your physical presence
- Build systems that generate revenue in your absence
- Transition from trading time for money to trading knowledge for money

The goal isn't just to be successful—it's to be so successful that you can bring others with you. Position yourself not just for personal elevation, but for the ability to elevate your entire community.

PART IV:
THE EMPIRE - BUILDING
MULTIPLE STREAMS

CHAPTER 9

COVID CHAOS & CASH OPPORTUNITIES

March 2020 changed everything overnight.

One day I was flying between cities teaching hair classes to packed rooms, running my storefront location for Billionaire's Hair in Hampton, Virginia at the Coliseum Crossing shopping center, and managing celebrity clients who needed their hair done for red carpet events. The next day, everything shut down.

No travel. No in-person classes. No events. No physical business operations.

For most people in the beauty industry, COVID was a death sentence for their income. Stylists couldn't work. Salons were closed. Beauty supply stores were deemed non-essential. The entire industry ground to a halt.

But here's what I'd learned from my years in the streets and in business: crisis always creates opportunity for people who are paying attention.

While everyone else was panicking about what they couldn't do anymore, I was asking myself a different question: What can I do now that I couldn't do before?

The answer was simple: I could finally focus entirely on digital.

For years, I'd been splitting my time between physical services and digital education. The physical work paid well, but it required my constant presence. The digital work had more potential for scale, but I'd never given it my full attention.

COVID forced my hand, and honestly, it was the best thing that could have happened to my business evolution.

Within the first month of lockdown, I pivoted completely to online education. I moved all my in-person hair classes to Zoom and Facebook Live. Instead of teaching 20-30 people in a hotel conference room, I was teaching hundreds of people simultaneously from my living room.

I created a monthly membership group for $99 where I taught advanced hair techniques, business strategies, and marketing tips. We were doing $100,000+ per month just from the digital education side of the business.

But the real breakthrough came when I realized that my hair business had actually been a marketing and customer psychology business disguised as a beauty business. All the skills I'd developed—understanding consumer behavior, building trust through content, creating urgency around limited offers, managing customer relationships at scale—those skills could be applied to any industry.

That's when I met the man who would change my financial trajectory forever, though not in the way I expected.

I'd started dating this guy who was deep in the scamming world in Atlanta. Now, I want to be clear: I wasn't going backward. I wasn't getting involved in illegal activities again. But I was curious about how the game had evolved since my time in it, and this man was teaching me about some of the newer methods.

One day he mentioned something about COVID business relief programs. Specifically, something called the COVID Relief Credit, which was a legitimate tax credit designed to help business owners who had lost revenue due to COVID.

"Business owners can get up to $30,000 back if they lost money because of COVID," he told me.

I stopped him right there. "Wait. Is this legal?"

"It's a government program," he said. "It's literally designed to help businesses that were hurt by the pandemic."

My mind started racing. I knew a lot of business owners who'd been devastated by COVID. Hair stylists, restaurant owners, small business operators—people who'd seen their income disappear overnight through no fault of their own.

But here was my problem: this man didn't really understand the program himself. He was just repeating what someone else had told him. If I was going to get involved in anything tax-related, I needed to understand it completely and make sure it was 100% legitimate.

So I started researching. Deep research. I read IRS publications, studied the actual tax code, consulted with CPAs, and made sure I understood every aspect of the Employee Retention Credit program.

What I discovered was incredible. This was a legitimate government program designed to help business owners recover financially from COVID-related losses. But most business owners didn't know about it, and the ones who did know about it didn't understand how to apply for it properly.

It was a massive opportunity to help people get money they were legally entitled to while building a sustainable business for myself.

I tested it on my own business first. Then I helped my daughter apply. Then Lita. Then a few other close friends. Every single application was approved, and people were getting $20,000, $30,000, sometimes more.

But I was still moving carefully. The last thing I wanted was to get involved in something that looked legitimate but had hidden legal problems. I'd already learned that lesson the hard way.

That's when my relationship with this man ended badly. We broke up right around my birthday—because apparently I have a pattern of evaluating my life every Cancer season and making major changes.

When we broke up, he said something that lit a fire under me that I didn't even know was there: "Figure out how you're gonna pay your rent."

He said it like he thought I was helpless without him, like I couldn't handle my own financial obligations, like I needed him to survive.

He was about to learn something about Cancer women that he should have researched before he tried me.

When a Cancer woman gets activated, she doesn't just get motivated—she gets obsessed. We don't just want to prove you wrong—we want to get a PhD in proving you wrong.

So I took that tax program and I went absolutely crazy with it.

I started with a simple strategy: I'll help you get your money back for $300, or I'll teach you how to do it yourself for $200.

The first person who paid me $300 opened the floodgates. Then another person. Then another. Word spread through my network, then through their networks.

Within weeks, I was making $10,000-$15,000 per day helping business owners get money back from the government. Money they were legally entitled to. Money that was just sitting there waiting for them to claim it, but they didn't know how.

Remember, this was July 2022. I had about $15,000 in monthly expenses between my rent, my lifestyle, and my business costs. In one good week, I was making more than my entire monthly overhead.

But it wasn't just about the money I was making. It was about the money I was helping other people get. These were real business owners who'd been struggling since COVID started. Hair stylists like I used to be. Restaurant owners who'd had to close down. Small business operators who'd lost everything and were trying to rebuild.

When they got $20,000-$30,000 back from the government, it wasn't just tax relief—it was life-changing money. It was catch-up-on-rent money. It was keep-the-lights-on money. It was restart-your-business money.

I realized I'd found my calling beyond just building personal wealth. I was helping people get money that belonged to them anyway, using skills I'd developed in completely different industries.

The first major validation came when my daughter got her $30,000 payment—on my grandmother's birthday, August 10th. That felt like a sign from heaven. Like my grandmother was saying, "This is it, baby. This is what you're supposed to be doing."

After that, it was payment after payment after payment. By September, I'd probably helped people get back over $500,000 from the government, and I'd made more money in two months than I'd made in some entire years.

But I knew I needed to get educated properly. I couldn't just be repeating what someone else had taught me. If I was going to be in the tax business, I needed to understand taxes at a professional level.

So I flew to Houston to take actual tax preparation courses. I studied everything I could get my hands on about business taxes, payroll taxes, and government relief programs. I turned myself into a legitimate tax professional, not just someone who knew about one program.

The tax business taught me something crucial about positioning: sometimes the best opportunities come from connecting people with resources they're already entitled to, not from creating new products or services.

The government had allocated billions of dollars to help small businesses recover from COVID. But there was a massive gap between the availability of these programs and business owners' knowledge about them. I became the bridge.

It also taught me about the power of timing. These COVID relief programs weren't going to last forever. There were deadlines, changing requirements, and limited windows of opportunity. Success wasn't just about knowing what to do—it was about acting fast while the opportunity was still available.

Most importantly, it showed me that my skills were completely transferable across industries. The same customer psychology, sales techniques, and marketing strategies that had made me successful in hair could make me successful in financial services.

The relationship that ended with "figure out how you're gonna pay your rent" had accidentally introduced me to the industry that would make me more money than everything else I'd done combined.

Sometimes your biggest breakthrough comes disguised as your worst breakup.

The tax business was just the beginning. But it taught me that there was serious money to be made helping people navigate complex financial systems, and that my background—understanding both struggle and success—gave me credibility with customers that traditional financial advisors couldn't match.

I wasn't just selling a service. I was selling hope, opportunity, and access to resources that could change people's lives.

And that was a business model I could scale infinitely.

BLUEPRINT LESSON: Crisis Creates Opportunity for the Prepared

COVID didn't create opportunities—it revealed them. Here's how to position yourself to profit during any crisis:

The Crisis Opportunity Formula:

1. **Identify what stopped working** (in-person services, traditional business models)
2. **Ask what became possible** (digital education, government programs, new consumer needs)
3. **Bridge the gap** between problems and solutions
4. **Move fast** while others are still paralyzed

Why Crisis Favors Entrepreneurs:

- **Flexibility Advantage**: Small businesses can pivot faster than large corporations
- **Reduced Competition**: Many people retreat during uncertainty, creating market gaps
- **Increased Need**: Crisis creates urgent problems that people will pay to solve
- **Lower Barriers**: Traditional gatekeepers are often disrupted, creating new pathways

The Digital Acceleration: COVID forced a 10-year digital transformation in 10 months:

- Online education exploded from niche to mainstream

- Digital payments became standard everywhere
- Remote services became acceptable across industries
- Social media became the primary marketing channel

Government Program Opportunities: During any crisis, governments create programs to help:

- Most people don't know about them
- Those who know don't understand how to access them
- There's always a gap between availability and utilization
- Being the bridge is extremely profitable

The Transferable Skills Advantage: Your skills from one industry always transfer to others:

- Customer psychology is universal
- Sales processes work across all businesses
- Marketing principles apply everywhere
- Relationship building translates to any field

Crisis Timing Strategy:

- **Phase 1 (Immediate)**: Focus on survival and helping others survive
- **Phase 2 (Adaptation)**: Identify new opportunities created by changed circumstances
- **Phase 3 (Growth)**: Scale the solutions that worked during adaptation
- **Phase 4 (Preparation)**: Build systems for the next inevitable crisis

The Credibility Factor: Your background during crisis becomes an asset:

- People trust those who've survived struggle
- Your story becomes proof that recovery is possible
- Your success gives others permission to believe in theirs
- Authenticity beats credentials during uncertain times

Key Questions for Any Crisis:

1. What do people need now that they didn't need before?
2. What resources exist that people don't know about?
3. What skills do I have that are more valuable now?
4. How can I serve while also building sustainable income?
5. What systems should I build now for the next opportunity?

Remember: Every crisis is temporary, but the habits and systems you build during crisis can create permanent wealth. Don't just survive the storm—use it to power your growth.

CHAPTER 10

TAXES, CREDIT & THE DIGITAL REVOLUTION

By the time 2022 rolled around, I was officially done with hair.

Not because the business wasn't profitable—it was still generating six figures annually. But because I'd found something bigger, something that could scale infinitely, something that aligned perfectly with my mission to help people build real wealth.

The tax business had opened my eyes to an entire world of financial opportunities that most people don't even know exist. And the more I learned about the tax code, the more I realized it wasn't just a set of rules—it was a wealth-building manual written in a language most people can't read.

The government literally publishes instructions on how to legally reduce your tax burden, create business deductions, and build generational wealth. But it's written in legal jargon that keeps 99% of people from accessing it.

I decided to become a translator.

The Employee Retention Credit had been just the beginning. As I dove deeper into tax education, I discovered dozens of legitimate strategies that business owners could use to keep more of their money and reinvest it into growth.

But here's what separated me from traditional tax professionals: I spoke the language of people who'd been locked out of traditional wealth-building systems.

Most CPAs and tax advisors come from middle-class backgrounds. They went to college, got their certifications, and built practices serving people who already had money. They could explain tax strategies to business owners who already understood business terminology and had existing relationships with financial professionals.

But what about the hair stylists working out of their kitchens? The food truck owners grinding to make ends meet? The former dancers trying to legitimize their hustle? The system-impacted entrepreneurs who couldn't get traditional business loans?

These people needed tax help too, but they needed it explained in a way they could understand, by someone who understood where they were coming from.

That became my niche: financial education for people who'd been excluded from traditional financial education.

I started creating content that broke down complex tax concepts into simple, actionable steps. Instead of talking about "depreciation schedules" and "section 179 deductions," I'd say, "Here's how to write off that car you bought for your business" and "This is how to turn your home office into a tax deduction."

The response was incredible. My social media engagement exploded. People were sharing my content, tagging their friends, and most importantly, they were implementing the strategies I was teaching.

But the real game-changer came when I discovered the credit repair industry.

Now, I need to be careful how I explain this, because there's a lot of misinformation and scammy behavior in the credit space. But there are also legitimate strategies for improving credit scores that most people don't know about.

I'd learned about credit management the hard way during my illegal days. When I got that CPN (Credit Privacy Number), I treated it like the Holy Grail because I knew how powerful good credit could be. I paid everything on time, kept my utilization low, and built an 800+ credit score that allowed me to get cars, apartments, and business funding that my real credit couldn't qualify for.

But what I realized later was that most of what I'd learned about credit building could be applied legally to help people improve their actual credit scores.

In 2023, a new credit dispute method called "the credit sweep" started making waves in the industry. This was different from traditional credit repair, which focused on disputing individual items. The credit sweep was a systematic approach that could remove multiple negative items simultaneously.

I saw an opportunity to do it better, more transparently, and more affordably.

I spent months researching the credit sweep method, understanding exactly how it worked, and figuring out how to implement it ethically. In June 2024, I connected with Tyrell Brown (@Chiefsbs on Instagram), who taught me not just credit sweeps, but most importantly, system automations that would transform how I delivered services. Then I started offering credit repair services alongside my tax services.

The combination was perfect. Tax strategies help people keep more money. Credit repair helps them access more money through better borrowing terms. Together, they create a complete financial transformation system.

But instead of just doing the services for people, I also taught them how to do it themselves. I created courses on credit repair, tax planning, and business funding that people could implement on their own or hire me to do for them.

This is where my background became my biggest asset. I could talk to a former drug dealer about business funding because I understood that mindset. I could explain credit building to a dancer because I'd been there. I could help a system-impacted person navigate business formation because I knew the challenges they were facing.

My credibility wasn't coming from degrees or certifications—it was coming from results and relatability.

The business model became incredibly powerful:

Level 1: Education - I'd create content teaching financial strategies, building my audience and establishing credibility.

Level 2: Courses - I'd offer in-depth training on specific topics like credit repair or tax planning for people who wanted to DIY.

Level 3: Services - I'd provide done-for-you services for people who wanted to pay me to handle everything.

Level 4: Mentorship - I'd teach other people how to build similar businesses, creating multiple revenue streams.

Each level fed into the next, and the profit margins were incredible compared to physical products or traditional services.

But the real breakthrough came when I started combining everything into a comprehensive business ecosystem.

Instead of just being a tax person or a credit person, I became the person who could help you build wealth from the ground up. I could help you start a business, structure it properly for tax advantages, build business credit, get funding, and scale operations.

I was offering something that traditional financial advisors couldn't: a complete wealth-building system designed specifically for people who'd been locked out of traditional systems.

The digital revolution made all of this possible. Through social media, I could reach thousands of people daily. Through online courses, I could teach people while I slept. Through automated systems, I could deliver services without being physically present.

But most importantly, through authentic storytelling, I could build trust with people who'd been burned by financial professionals before.

I wasn't just selling services—I was selling transformation. I was showing people that their background didn't disqualify them from building wealth, that their mistakes could become their expertise, that their struggle could become their strength.

The numbers were staggering. Between tax services, credit repair, business consulting, and educational products, I was generating multiple six figures monthly. But more importantly, I was helping thousands of people improve their financial situations.

I had clients getting $50,000 back in tax refunds. Credit clients seeing 100+ point improvements in their scores. Business clients securing six-figure funding deals. Women who'd been dancing or struggling financially were building legitimate businesses and generational wealth.

That's when I realized I wasn't just running businesses—I was running a movement.

The digital revolution had given people like me the ability to compete with traditional institutions. We didn't need expensive offices or institutional backing. We just needed expertise, authenticity, and the ability to connect with people who looked like us and came from where we came from.

My prison promise to use whatever platform I was given to bring others with me was finally being fulfilled on a scale I'd never imagined.

But success at this level comes with new challenges. The bigger your platform, the more scrutiny you face. The more money you make, the more people want to tear you down. The more you help people, the more responsibility you feel to get everything perfect.

I had to learn how to handle success without losing the authenticity that had made me successful in the first place. I had to figure out how to scale impact without sacrificing quality. I had to navigate the complex world of online business while staying true to my mission of helping people who'd been left behind by traditional systems.

The digital revolution had given me the tools to build an empire. But building an empire meant taking on the responsibilities that come with that level of influence and impact.

I was no longer just Barbie from Outeast trying to make it out. I was Billionaire Barbie, with a platform, a responsibility, and the power to change lives on a massive scale.

The question became: What was I going to do with all of that power?

BOSS TIP: The Tax Code is a Wealth Manual for Those Who Read It

Most people see taxes as something that happens TO them. Wealthy people understand that taxes are something you can strategically plan AROUND. Here's how to shift your mindset:

The Tax Code Reality:

- The tax code isn't designed to punish you—it's designed to incentive certain behaviors
- Every deduction, credit, and strategy is legally published and available to everyone
- The wealthy stay wealthy partly because they understand how to legally minimize taxes
- What looks like "loopholes" are actually intentional policy designed to stimulate economic activity

Key Wealth-Building Tax Strategies:

1. **Business Structure Optimization**: LLC vs. S-Corp vs. sole proprietorship can save thousands annually
2. **Business Expense Maximization**: Turn personal expenses into legitimate business deductions
3. **Retirement Account Strategies**: Traditional vs. Roth vs. SEP-IRA based on your situation
4. **Real Estate Investment Benefits**: Depreciation, 1031 exchanges, and passive loss advantages
5. **Tax Credit Harvesting**: R&D credits, work opportunity credits, and industry-specific incentives

The Credit-Tax Connection: Good credit amplifies tax strategies:

- Business credit allows you to invest without personal liability
- Real estate investments (prime tax advantages) require good credit
- Equipment financing for business purchases creates immediate deductions
- Lines of credit provide cash flow for tax-advantaged investments

Why DIY Education Matters: Even if you hire professionals, understand the basics:

- You can't verify advice you don't understand
- Tax professionals make mistakes when you're not informed
- Knowledge allows you to ask better questions and make better decisions
- Understanding the rules helps you spot opportunities others miss

The Wealth Building Sequence:

1. **Learn the rules** (tax code basics, credit fundamentals)
2. **Structure properly** (business formation, banking setup)
3. **Implement strategies** (deductions, credit building, tax planning)
4. **Scale systematically** (reinvest savings, leverage credit for growth)
5. **Teach others** (education creates additional revenue streams)

Red Flags to Avoid:

- Anyone promising "secrets" the IRS doesn't want you to know
- Strategies that seem too good to be true (they usually are)
- Advisors who can't explain strategies in simple terms

- Services that don't provide documentation or proof of legitimacy

The Mindset Shift: Stop thinking: "How do I pay less taxes?" Start thinking: "How do I structure my finances to legally optimize my tax situation while building wealth?"

Resources for Self-Education:

- IRS publications (boring but authoritative)
- Reputable tax education courses
- Books by established tax professionals
- Software like TurboTax for learning basic concepts

Remember: The tax code is thousands of pages long because it contains thousands of opportunities. The wealthy use tax strategies not to avoid paying their fair share, but to keep more of their money working for them instead of for the government.

Your education is your best investment. The more you understand about taxes and credit, the more money you can legally keep and strategically deploy for wealth building.

CHAPTER 11

PERSONAL BRAND
= PERSONAL POWER

The day I realized my personal brand was more valuable than any business I could ever build was the day everything changed.

It happened during a conversation with a client who'd paid me $5,000 for credit repair services. After I'd successfully removed several negative items from her credit report and improved her score by over 100 points, she said something that stopped me in my tracks:

"I didn't hire you because you were the best credit repair person I could find. I hired you because you're the only one who made me believe I could actually change my life."

That's when it hit me: people weren't just buying my services. They were buying my story, my energy, my proof that transformation was possible. They were buying hope from someone who looked like them, came from where they came from, and had overcome what they were trying to overcome.

My personal brand wasn't just marketing—it was my greatest business asset.

But building a personal brand as someone with my background wasn't simple. I had to figure out how to be authentic about my past without letting it define my future. I had to be vulnerable enough to connect with people while still maintaining the credibility needed to charge premium prices.

Most importantly, I had to learn the difference between transparency and oversharing, between being real and being reckless.

The breakthrough came when I stopped trying to hide my story and started using it strategically.

Instead of trying to present myself as someone who'd always been successful, I leaned into being someone who'd transformed their life completely. Instead of competing with people who had traditional credentials, I positioned myself as the alternative for people who'd been failed by traditional systems.

My tagline became "From Felon to Fortune" long before this book existed, because that journey was my differentiator in a crowded market.

But personal branding isn't just about having a compelling story—it's about consistently delivering value in a way that only you can deliver it.

I developed what I call my "transparency framework":

Level 1: Share the lesson, not just the struggle. When I talked about my criminal past, I always connected it to a business principle or life lesson that people could apply immediately.

Level 2: Show the process, not just the results. Instead of just posting about my success, I documented the actual work—the research, the failures, the problem-solving that led to breakthrough moments.

Level 3: Serve the community, not just the customer. I created content that helped people even if they never bought anything from me, building trust and goodwill that eventually converted to sales.

Level 4: Stay connected to your origin story. No matter how successful I became, I never forgot where I came from or stopped serving people who reminded me of my former self.

This framework allowed me to build something that traditional businesses struggle to create: a loyal community that felt personally invested in my success.

I called them my "Rich Cousins," and they became the foundation of everything I built.

These weren't just customers or followers—they were men & women who saw themselves in my story and wanted to be part of my journey. They shared my content, defended me against critics, referred their friends, and created a word-of-mouth marketing machine that no advertising budget could have bought.

But building this community required a level of vulnerability that most business owners aren't comfortable with.

I shared the good and the bad. When I made a quarter-million dollars in three days, I posted about it. When I lost a quarter-million dollars due to a bad supplier, I posted about that too. When I was struggling with relationship issues, business challenges, or personal growth, I talked about it openly.

This level of transparency did two things: it built incredible trust with my audience, and it scared away people who weren't really aligned with my mission anyway.

The result was a highly engaged, fiercely loyal community that converted at rates traditional marketing experts said were impossible.

But the real magic happened when I started merging my business brand with my personal brand completely.

For years, I'd been running "Billionaires Hair" as a separate entity from "Billionaire Barbie." The business had its own social media accounts, its own branding, its own identity. But what I realized was that people were connecting with me, not with the business.

So I made a strategic decision that most business advisors would have called crazy: I merged everything under my personal brand.

"Billionaires Hair" became "I Am Billionaire Barbie." All the business accounts were consolidated into my personal accounts. Every service, every product, every course was positioned as coming directly from me, not from some faceless corporation.

This decision multiplied my impact and income almost immediately.

When you're selling a service from a business, people can comparison shop. When you're selling expertise from a personal brand, you have no direct competition because nobody else has your exact story, perspective, and approach.

But personal branding at this level comes with unique challenges.

Challenge #1: Scaling without losing authenticity. As my audience grew from thousands to hundreds of thousands, I had to figure out how to maintain personal connection with people I couldn't personally respond to anymore.

Challenge #2: Managing public criticism. The bigger your platform, the more people want to tear you down. I had to develop thick skin and strategic responses to handle both legitimate criticism and outright hate.

Challenge #3: Protecting your energy. When your brand is built on being accessible and relatable, people expect unlimited access to you. I had to learn to set boundaries without seeming fake or corporate.

Challenge #4: Staying grounded in success. When you're making millions and being celebrated constantly, it's easy to lose touch with the humility and hunger that made you successful in the first place.

The solution to all of these challenges was developing what I call "intentional authenticity."

Instead of sharing everything all the time, I became strategic about what I shared, when I shared it, and how I framed it. I stayed real and relatable while also maintaining the boundaries necessary to protect my energy and my business.

I also became obsessed with the language I used. Every word mattered because every word was being scrutinized by thousands of people.

Instead of saying "good morning," I'd say "rich risings." Instead of asking "how are you doing?" I'd ask "how abundant are you?" Instead of casual conversation, every interaction became an opportunity to reinforce abundance mindset and positive energy.

This wasn't fake—it was intentional. I was using my platform to program not just my audience's minds, but my own mind for success and abundance.

The personal branding strategy that emerged from all of this became the template I now teach to other entrepreneurs:

1. Own your story completely. Don't hide from your past—use it as your competitive advantage.

2. Serve before you sell. Provide massive value to people who can't afford to pay you, and they'll become your biggest advocates.

3. Be consistently you. People can spot fake authenticity from a mile away. It's better to be genuinely imperfect than perfectly fake.

4. Document everything. Your journey is content. Your mistakes are lessons. Your successes are inspiration. Share it all strategically.

5. Build community, not just customers. People who feel connected to your mission will support you through anything.

The most powerful part of building a strong personal brand is that it becomes transferable across any industry or business model.

When I pivoted from hair to taxes, my audience came with me. When I added credit repair, they were interested because I was offering it. When I started business consulting, they wanted to learn because they trusted my expertise.

A product-based brand can't do that. If you build a successful hair company and want to start selling financial services, you're starting from scratch. But when you build a personal brand based on transformation, expertise, and authentic connection, you can take that audience anywhere.

This is why I always tell new entrepreneurs: build your personal brand first, then build businesses around it. Your personal brand will outlast any individual business, and it will give you the flexibility to pivot, evolve, and grow without losing your foundation.

The girl who used to hide behind stage names and fake identities had learned that her real name, real story, and real personality were her greatest assets.

Billionaire Barbie wasn't just a business name—it was a movement, a mindset, and a community of women who believed that their past didn't determine their future.

And that community was about to become the foundation for something bigger than I'd ever imagined.

BLUEPRINT LESSON: Your Story is Your Greatest Asset

In a world where everyone can access the same information, tools, and strategies, your unique story becomes your only true competitive advantage. Here's how to turn your personal narrative into business power:

The Authenticity Advantage:

- Your struggles make you relatable to people facing similar challenges

- Your transformation proves that change is possible
- Your current success gives people permission to believe in their own potential
- Your mistakes become case studies that help others avoid the same pitfalls

The Transparency Framework:

1. **Context First**: Always provide the lesson or principle before sharing personal details
2. **Value Always**: Every personal story should teach something actionable
3. **Boundaries Matter**: Share strategically, not compulsively
4. **Progress Over Perfection**: Show growth, not just arrival

Building Your Personal Brand Platform:

- **Consistency**: Same message, energy, and values across all platforms
- **Frequency**: Regular content that keeps you top-of-mind
- **Value**: Every piece of content should help, inspire, or educate
- **Personality**: Let your real character shine through professional presentation

The Community Building Strategy:

1. **Serve First**: Help people before asking for anything
2. **Engage Genuinely**: Respond personally when possible
3. **Create Belonging**: Make people feel part of something bigger
4. **Celebrate Others**: Highlight your community's successes

5. **Stay Accessible**: Never become too big to connect with your people

Monetizing Personal Brand:

- **Direct Services**: People pay premium for personal expertise
- **Educational Products**: Your knowledge becomes scalable income
- **Speaking/Consulting**: Your story becomes valuable content for others
- **Affiliate/Partnerships**: Companies want access to your audience
- **Product Endorsements**: Your recommendation carries weight with your community

Managing Growth Challenges:

- **Energy Protection**: Set clear boundaries about availability
- **Quality Control**: Don't scale so fast you lose personal connection
- **Criticism Management**: Develop responses to both valid feedback and baseless attacks
- **Team Building**: Hire people who understand and can represent your brand values

The Long-Term View: Personal brands compound over time:

- Your reputation grows with every positive interaction
- Your expertise deepens with every challenge you overcome
- Your audience becomes more valuable as it grows and ages with you

- Your story becomes more powerful as you achieve bigger goals

Common Personal Branding Mistakes:

- Trying to be everything to everyone
- Hiding struggles to appear perfect
- Copying other people's voice instead of developing your own
- Focusing on follower count instead of engagement quality
- Selling too much without providing enough value

The Ultimate Personal Brand Question: "If someone could buy expertise from anyone in your field, why would they choose YOU specifically?"

Your answer to that question should be rooted in your unique story, approach, and connection with your audience. When you can answer that clearly, you've found your personal brand positioning.

Remember: In business, people don't just buy products or services—they buy the person behind them. Make sure that person is authentically, strategically, and powerfully YOU.

PART V:
THE ELEVATION
- LEGACY & BEYOND

CHAPTER 12

FROM SCAMMER TO SAVIOR - REDEMPTION ECONOMICS

The message came through my DMs on a Tuesday morning, and it stopped me cold:

"Barbie, I was about to go back to the pole tonight because my rent is due tomorrow and I'm broke. Then I watched your story about building credit, applied what you taught, and got approved for a $10,000 business line of credit this morning. I'm not going back to dancing. Thank you for saving my life."

I sat there staring at my phone, tears running down my face, because this was exactly why I'd made that promise to God in prison. This was the purpose behind all the success, all the platform building, all the wealth creation.

I wasn't just running businesses anymore. I was running rescue missions.

But let me back up and explain how I got to this point, because the journey from scammer to savior wasn't automatic—it was intentional.

After I'd built my tax and credit businesses to consistent seven-figure revenue, I had a choice to make. I could keep scaling for personal wealth, focusing on high-paying clients and premium services. Or I could use my platform to systematically help people who reminded me of my former self.

I chose mission over money, though as it turned out, mission became the foundation for even more money.

See, there's something beautiful about God: when you align your business with your purpose, everything flows easier. When you're genuinely trying to help people transform their lives, they sense that authenticity and trust you with their transformation.

But before I could help anyone else, I had to confront something uncomfortable: the full scope of harm I'd caused during my illegal years.

I had to think about the people whose identities I'd stolen, the businesses I'd defrauded, the community trust I'd violated. I had to face the fact that while I was getting my life together, I'd left damage in my wake that I could never fully repair.

That reckoning led me to what I call "redemption economics"—the idea that you can't undo your past, but you can use your future to create more good than harm you originally caused.

For every dollar I'd stolen, I committed to helping someone legitimately earn ten dollars. For every person I'd hurt through fraud, I committed to helping ten people build legitimate wealth. For every system I'd exploited illegally, I committed to teaching people how to use those same systems legally.

This wasn't just guilt-driven charity. This was strategic purpose that made my business more powerful and more profitable than pure profit-seeking ever could have.

The first group I focused on was obvious: former dancers and sex workers trying to transition to legitimate income.

These women face unique challenges that traditional business coaches don't understand. They're used to making money immediately, so the slow build of legitimate business feels impossible. They often have no traditional work history or references. Many have tax complications from cash-based income they never reported.

But they also have incredible business skills that they don't even recognize: customer psychology, sales ability, marketing instincts, financial management, and the hustle mentality that every entrepreneur needs.

My job became helping them see their existing skills as assets while teaching them how to channel those skills legally.

I started offering special programs specifically for women transitioning out of the adult industry. Credit repair to help them qualify for apartments and business funding. Tax guidance to help them get right with the IRS. Business formation to help them legitimize their income streams.

But most importantly, I provided them with proof that the transition was possible. When they looked at me, they saw someone who'd been where they were and built something legitimate. They couldn't use education or traditional networking to disqualify my advice because I'd walked their exact path.

The results were incredible. Women who'd been making $500-$1000 per night dancing learned to make $30K per month with legitimate businesses. Former sex workers became successful entrepreneurs, credit repair specialists, tax preparers, and business consultants. Former inmates transitioned from the streets to boardrooms, building legitimate enterprises that created generational wealth instead of generational trauma.

Each success story became content for my platform, which attracted more women who needed help, which created more success stories. It became a virtuous cycle of transformation that grew my business while fulfilling my mission.

Then I expanded to the second group: formerly incarcerated people trying to rebuild their lives.

The system-impacted community faces challenges that go beyond just employment discrimination. They have gaps in their work history that are hard to explain. They often lack the professional networks that lead to opportunities. Many have damaged credit from being unable to pay bills while incarcerated.

But like the dancers, they also have skills that aren't recognized by traditional society: resilience, resourcefulness, the ability to navigate complex systems, and the motivation that comes from knowing what it's like to lose everything.

I started creating content specifically about building businesses with a criminal background. How to structure businesses to minimize background check issues. How to rebuild credit after incarceration. How to turn your story into an asset instead of a liability.

I also started speaking at reentry programs, halfway houses, and community organizations. Not just motivational speaking, but tactical education about specific steps people could take to build legitimate wealth.

The third group happened organically: people in the streets who were tired of illegal income but didn't know how to transition.

These were active hustlers who followed me on social media, watched my content, and started asking questions about going legitimate. Drug dealers wanting to understand business licensing. Scammers interested in learning legal ways to make money. People who were good at illegal sales wanting to learn legal sales.

This was the most sensitive group to work with because I had to be careful not to glorify illegal activity while still relating to their current reality. I couldn't tell them to just stop what they were doing without providing viable alternatives.

So I developed what I call "transition strategies"—ways to gradually shift from illegal to legal income streams without creating financial crisis.

For example, someone making money through credit card fraud could learn legitimate credit repair and use their understanding of credit systems to help people legally. Someone making money selling drugs could learn about legal business formation and use their sales skills to build legitimate enterprises.

The key was showing them that the skills that made them successful illegally could make them even more successful legally, with less risk and more sustainable growth.

But helping these communities wasn't just about individual transformation—it was about breaking generational cycles.

When a former dancer becomes a successful entrepreneur, she shows her daughter that there are other options. When a formerly incarcerated person builds legitimate wealth, they prove to their community that the system can be navigated legally. When someone transitions from the streets to business ownership, they create a new template for success.

This work became so central to my mission that I restructured all my businesses around it. Instead of just offering services to anyone who could pay, I made sure a percentage of my services were always available to people transitioning from illegal to legal income streams.

I created scholarship programs for my courses. I offered payment plans that made my services accessible to people rebuilding their finances. I partnered with reentry organizations and community groups to provide free workshops.

But the most powerful part was the community that formed around this mission. Former dancers started referring other dancers. Formerly incarcerated people started bringing their friends to my programs. People who'd successfully transitioned started helping others who were just beginning the journey.

My "Rich Cousins" community became a support network for women from all backgrounds who were transforming their lives. The single mother working two jobs learned alongside the former stripper building her first business and the formerly incarcerated woman starting her credit repair company.

This diversity made the community stronger and more powerful. Everyone brought different skills, perspectives, and networks. Everyone learned from everyone else's journey.

The financial results of this mission-driven approach were staggering. Within two years of focusing on redemption economics, my business revenue doubled. But more importantly, I was tracking transformation metrics that mattered more than money:

- Over 500 women had transitioned from adult entertainment to legitimate businesses
- More than 200 formerly incarcerated people had started successful enterprises
- Hundreds of people had improved their credit scores by 100+ points
- Thousands had learned to use tax strategies to legally keep more of their money

Each success story became proof that transformation was possible, which attracted more people who needed help, which created more success stories.

But the real validation came in unexpected moments. Like running into former clients at upscale restaurants, hearing about their children's college graduations, getting wedding invitations from women who'd found love after finding themselves.

Or like the message I mentioned at the beginning of this chapter—from a woman who was literally on her way back to a life she'd left behind, until my content reminded her that she had other options.

That's when I fully understood what redemption economics really means: when you transform your pain into purpose, your mess into your message, and your wounds into wisdom, you don't just heal yourself—you become a healing force for everyone who comes after you.

The girl who used to exploit systems illegally had become a woman who helped others navigate those same systems legally. The former criminal had become a legitimate business owner who created opportunities for other former criminals.

I couldn't change what I'd done in my past. But I could use what I'd learned from my past to change other people's futures.

And that's exactly what redemption economics is all about.

BOSS TIP: Your Darkest Moments Can Become Your Brightest Light

The experiences you're most ashamed of can become your greatest source of credibility and impact. Here's how to transform pain into purpose and mistakes into mission:

The Redemption Framework:

1. **Take Full Inventory**
   - Acknowledge the harm you caused (to yourself and others)
   - Identify the skills you developed (even through negative experiences)

- ○ Recognize the people who could benefit from your journey
- ○ Accept responsibility without drowning in shame

2. **Calculate Your Contribution**
   - ○ For every person you hurt, commit to helping multiple people
   - ○ For every dollar you took illegally, commit to helping people earn more legally
   - ○ For every system you exploited, commit to teaching legal navigation
   - ○ Set specific metrics for positive impact

3. **Identify Your Natural Audience**
   - ○ Who is facing the same challenges you once faced?
   - ○ Who has the same background but lacks the knowledge you've gained?
   - ○ Who would trust your advice because you've walked their path?
   - ○ Who needs to see that transformation is possible?

Why Mission-Driven Business Works Better:

- **Authentic Connection**: People sense when you genuinely care vs. just want their money
- **Natural Content**: Your transformation story becomes endless valuable content
- **Word-of-Mouth Marketing**: People share stories of hope more than they share product reviews
- **Sustainable Motivation**: Purpose-driven work energizes you during difficult times

- **Compound Impact**: Every person you help becomes proof that others can transform too

Common Transition Challenges:

- **Imposter Syndrome**: "Who am I to help anyone when I made so many mistakes?"
- **Perfectionism**: Waiting until you have it all figured out before helping others
- **Guilt Management**: Feeling like you don't deserve success because of your past
- **Credibility Questions**: People questioning your qualifications or motives

Overcoming Transition Obstacles:

1. **Use Your Story Strategically**: Share enough to build credibility, not so much that it becomes the focus
2. **Focus on Results**: Let your clients' transformations speak louder than your credentials
3. **Stay Connected to Your Why**: Remember the promise you made when you were at your lowest
4. **Build Incrementally**: Start with small acts of service and scale as you grow

The Business Benefits of Redemption Economics:

- Higher customer loyalty (people you've genuinely helped become lifelong advocates)
- Better referral rates (transformation stories inspire others to seek help)

- Premium pricing (people pay more for authentic expertise than academic knowledge)
- Sustainable growth (mission-driven businesses weather economic storms better)
- Personal fulfillment (making money while making a difference creates lasting satisfaction)

Creating Your Redemption Strategy:

1. **Define Your Target Impact**: Who specifically do you want to help?
2. **Develop Your Unique Approach**: How does your background create unique value?
3. **Create Accessible Entry Points**: How can people with limited resources access your help?
4. **Track Transformation Metrics**: Measure impact beyond just revenue
5. **Build Community**: Connect people you're helping with each other
6. **Scale Systematically**: Grow your capacity to help more people effectively

The Ultimate Test: Your redemption is complete when someone says: "I chose you not despite your past, but because of what you've done with your past."

Remember: The depth of your pit determines the height of your platform. The darker your background, the brighter your light can shine for others walking through similar darkness.

Your past mistakes don't disqualify you from helping others—they're exactly what qualifies you to help others avoid or overcome similar mistakes.

CHAPTER 13

BUILDING GENERATIONAL WEALTH & BREAKING CURSES

When my oldest daughter was 17, I finally told her the full truth about my past—the prison time she thought was job corps, the dancing, the illegal activities, all of it. After I shared my complete story, she looked at me with a mixture of shock and determination and said, "Mom, I had no idea you went through all that. But I'm glad you did, because it led to everything we have now. And I'm going to make sure my kids never have to wonder where their next opportunity is coming from."

That moment made me realize that everything I'd built wasn't just about my transformation. It was about creating a new normal for everyone who came after me.

See, generational wealth isn't just about leaving money to your children. It's about leaving them with the knowledge, connections, and mindset they need to create and maintain wealth for themselves. It's about changing the entire trajectory of your family tree.

When I was in prison writing those goals, I'd written about breaking generational curses. At the time, I was thinking about not getting pregnant as a teenager like my mother and grandmother had. I was thinking about not getting caught up in cycles of poverty and crime.

But what I understand now is that breaking generational curses requires more than just avoiding the mistakes of previous generations. It requires actively creating new patterns, new expectations, and new possibilities.

Let me tell you what generational poverty looked like in my family:

My grandmother had me and my mother young. They worked multiple jobs but never owned businesses. They made money but never built wealth. They survived but never thrived. They loved fiercely but never learned to heal their trauma, so they passed it down through volatile communication patterns and emotional dysregulation.

The family dynamics were complicated. My grandfather was a provider—he handled his business—but he had a temper that made the house tense sometimes. The women were strong but often carried emotional burdens that showed up in how we handled conflict. Money was always a source of stress, never a tool for freedom.

Success meant getting by. Wealth was something other people had. Education was something that might help you get a good job, not something that could help you create your own opportunities.

These weren't moral failings—these were the limitations of their circumstances, their education, and their environment. But limitations become generational when they're not consciously interrupted.

My transformation began the interruption, but it wasn't complete until I started teaching my children to think differently about everything.

Money Mindset Transformation:

Instead of teaching my children that money is hard to get and easy to lose, I taught them that money is abundant and flows to people who provide value to others.

Instead of teaching them to save every penny because you never know when hard times will come, I taught them to invest intelligently because money should work harder than they do.

Instead of teaching them that rich people are greedy or lucky, I taught them that wealthy people understand systems and strategies that can be learned by anyone willing to study.

Business Ownership as Normal:

My children grew up watching me build businesses, not just work for other people. They saw me create income streams, manage employees, solve problems, and scale operations. To them, entrepreneurship isn't scary or unusual—it's normal.

When my daughter was 16, she started her own small business selling products to her classmates. She did work a few jobs as a server to gain experience, but she quickly realized that building her own wealth creates more security than working for someone else's wealth. Now she's fully committed to her entrepreneurial journey because she understands the power of ownership over employment.

Education as Investment, Not Expense:

I changed how my family thinks about education completely. Instead of viewing college as the only path to success, I taught my children to view education as one tool among many for building the life they want.

My daughter is going to college, but not because she needs a degree to survive. She's going because she wants specific knowledge that will help her build the empire she's already envisioning. She understands that education should serve her goals, not define them.

More importantly, I taught her that the most valuable education happens outside of classrooms. Learning sales, understanding human psychology, developing emotional intelligence, building financial literacy—these skills matter more than any degree.

Network and Relationship Building:

My children grew up around successful people. They've been in business meetings, conference calls, and strategy sessions since they were young. They've met entrepreneurs, investors, and industry leaders as part of their normal environment.

This means they don't see successful people as different species. They understand that wealthy, powerful people are just people who've learned certain skills and principles. They have access to networks and relationships that would have taken me decades to build.

Trauma Healing and Emotional Intelligence:

Perhaps most importantly, I made sure my children had access to therapy, coaching, and emotional support that I never had. I didn't want them to spend their twenties and thirties healing from childhood trauma like I did.

I taught them healthy communication patterns, emotional regulation, and conflict resolution skills. I showed them how to process difficult emotions without numbing them with substances or destructive behaviors.

I also made sure they understood their family history—the good and the bad—so they could make conscious choices about what patterns to continue and what patterns to break.

The Ripple Effect:

But generational wealth building doesn't stop with your own children. It's about creating opportunities for everyone in your extended network who's ready to receive them.

I've hired family members in my businesses, teaching them skills and giving them experience they couldn't get elsewhere. I've funded business ventures for relatives who had good ideas but no capital. I've connected people in my network with opportunities that changed their financial trajectory.

I've also been strategic about the communities I support. When I do speaking engagements at schools, community centers, or reentry programs, I'm not just inspiring individuals—I'm introducing new possibilities to entire communities.

Every young woman who sees me speak and realizes she can build wealth without compromising her values changes not just her life, but potentially the lives of her future children. Every formerly incarcerated person who learns to build legitimate businesses becomes a model for others in their community.

This is how generational change happens: one family at a time, one community at a time, one transformed life at a time.

The Financial Infrastructure:

But mindset changes without financial infrastructure don't create lasting wealth. So I've also been building the actual financial foundation that my family can build on for generations.

Multiple businesses that generate passive income. Real estate investments that appreciate over time. Investment accounts that compound through market growth. Business structures that can be passed down and scaled by future generations.

I've also created educational trusts and scholarship funds that will help other young people get access to the kind of opportunities my children now take for granted.

Most importantly, I've documented everything. My children understand exactly how I built each business, what strategies worked, what mistakes to avoid, and how to replicate and improve on my results.

The Legacy Mindset:

Everything I do now is filtered through this question: "How will this decision affect my family for the next 100 years?"

That changes how you think about money, relationships, business partnerships, and even personal behavior. When you know your choices will impact people you'll never meet, you make different choices.

It also changes how you think about success. Personal achievement feels hollow when it doesn't create opportunities for others. True success means lifting as you climb, creating as you climb, and building ladders for people who are still down in the pit you climbed out of.

The Ultimate Breakthrough:

The ultimate breakthrough in generational wealth building came when I realized that my story wasn't just about me overcoming my circumstances. It was about me becoming the ancestor that my future generations would thank.

Somewhere in the future, there's a little girl who will grow up never knowing what it feels like to worry about money because of the foundation I'm building now. There's a young woman who will start her first business with capital, connections, and confidence because of the work I'm doing today.

There are communities that will be transformed because of the businesses I'm building, the people I'm training, and the examples I'm setting right now.

When I think about it that way, every sacrifice makes sense. Every late night working becomes an investment in someone's future freedom. Every dollar I reinvest instead of spending becomes someone's inheritance. Every person I help becomes someone who can help others.

My daughter often tells me she wants to be just like me, but what she doesn't realize is that she's already surpassed me in so many ways. She'll never think like I used to think. She'll never accept limitations that I used to accept. She'll never operate from the scarcity mindset that I had to overcome.

She represents the first generation of wealth builders in our family instead of the first generation of wealth earners.

And that's the difference between breaking generational poverty and building generational wealth.

Breaking generational poverty means you escape. Building generational wealth means everyone who comes after you starts from a higher platform than you did.

That's the legacy I'm building. That's the fortune that matters most.

The girl from Outeast who used to point at drug dealers as examples of success is now the woman her great-great-granddaughter will point to as the one who changed everything.

That transformation didn't happen by accident. It happened by intention, strategy, and the understanding that your current choices become your future generations' starting point.

Choose accordingly.

BLUEPRINT LESSON: True Wealth Outlives You

Building generational wealth requires thinking beyond your own lifetime and creating systems that serve people you'll never meet. Here's the framework for legacy building:

The Four Pillars of Generational Wealth:

1. Financial Infrastructure

- Multiple income streams that can operate without your direct involvement
- Assets that appreciate faster than inflation (real estate, investments, businesses)
- Legal structures that protect wealth and minimize taxes across generations
- Insurance and estate planning that preserves wealth during transitions

2. Knowledge Transfer

- Document your processes, strategies, and lessons learned
- Teach business principles, not just hand over money
- Create educational systems that prepare future generations to manage wealth
- Share both your successes and failures as learning tools

3. Network and Relationship Capital

- Introduce your children to successful people and environments
- Build connections that create opportunities across industries

- Develop relationships that span generations
- Create access to rooms, resources, and opportunities

4. Mindset and Values Transformation

- Change how your family thinks about money, work, and success
- Heal generational trauma that sabotages financial progress
- Establish new patterns of communication and conflict resolution
- Create family cultures that support growth and achievement

Breaking Limiting Generational Patterns:

Common Patterns to Interrupt:

- "Money is the root of all evil" vs. "Money is a tool for good"
- "Rich people are greedy" vs. "Wealthy people solve problems for others"
- "You have to work hard for money" vs. "You can work smart with money"
- "Save every penny" vs. "Invest intelligently for growth"
- "Don't get too big for your britches" vs. "Aim higher than anyone expects"

The Legacy Planning Process:

1. **Assess Current Patterns**: What limiting beliefs and behaviors run in your family?
2. **Define New Standards**: What do you want the next generation to consider normal?
3. **Create Education Systems**: How will you transfer knowledge and wisdom?

4. **Build Financial Infrastructure**: What assets will compound over generations?
5. **Document Everything**: What should future generations know about your journey?

Teaching Wealth Principles to Children:

Age 5-10: Basic money concepts, entrepreneurship games, value creation **Age 11-15**: Business fundamentals, investment basics, financial literacy **Age 16-18**: Real business experience, advanced strategies, network building **Age 18+**: Partnership opportunities, independent ventures, legacy planning

The Community Impact Model: True generational wealth extends beyond your family:

- Invest in your community's educational and economic development
- Create job opportunities for people from similar backgrounds
- Fund scholarships and mentorship programs
- Support businesses owned by people from marginalized communities

Measuring Generational Success:

- Do your children understand business and investing?
- Can they create income without traditional employment?
- Do they have access to networks and opportunities you didn't have?
- Are they positioned to build on your foundation rather than starting over?

- Will their children grow up with even more advantages?

The Ultimate Legacy Question: "What would someone have to leave you for your life to be completely transformed?"

Now work backward: What do you need to build so that your great-grandchildren inherit that level of life transformation?

Common Legacy Building Mistakes:

- Giving money without teaching money management
- Building businesses without creating succession plans
- Focusing only on financial inheritance while ignoring mindset inheritance
- Trying to control future generations instead of empowering them
- Building wealth for yourself first instead of building wealth for generations

Remember: Generational wealth isn't about how much money you leave—it's about how much opportunity you create. The goal isn't to make your children dependent on your wealth, but to make them capable of building their own wealth at levels you can't even imagine.

Your legacy isn't what you accumulate—it's what you activate in the people who come after you.

CONCLUSION

YOUR BILLIONAIRE BLUEPRINT

I 'm writing this conclusion from my gated mini mansion in Buckhead that I once could only dream about—the same area where I used to look up at the luxury homes from the streets of Atlanta, wondering what kind of person got to live in such beautiful places.

Outside my window, the city sprawls beneath me like a map of possibilities. Somewhere down there is a young woman making the same desperate choices I once made. Somewhere out there is a person sitting in a cell, writing goals on a piece of paper like I did. Somewhere in this city is someone who needs to hear that their past doesn't determine their future.

This book isn't just my story—it's your invitation.

An invitation to stop letting your circumstances define your possibilities. An invitation to transform your pain into your power, your mess into your message, your wounds into your wisdom. An invitation to build something so much bigger than survival.

But let me be clear about something: reading this book won't change your life. Knowledge without action is just entertainment. Inspiration without implementation is just motivation that fades when reality hits.

Your transformation starts when you close this book and ask yourself one question: "What am I going to do differently starting today?"

Because everything I've shared with you—every strategy, every principle, every blueprint lesson—only works if you work it.

The Blueprint is Simple (But Not Easy):

1. **Own your story completely.** Stop running from your past and start running with it. Your background is your differentiation, not your disqualification.

2. **Serve before you sell.** Help people even when they can't pay you. Build trust through value, not just through marketing.

3. **Think bigger than yourself.** Your success should create opportunities for others. Your platform should lift people up, not just lift you up.

4. **Build systems, not just income.** Create businesses that work without you. Develop passive income streams that compound over time.

5. **Invest in yourself relentlessly.** Your education is your best investment. Your mindset is your greatest asset.

6. **Write the vision and make it plain.** Document your goals, review them daily, and adjust them as you grow.

7. **Favor isn't fair, but it's real.** When opportunities come, be prepared to receive them. When doors open, be ready to walk through them.

The Truth About Transformation:

It's messier than the success stories make it seem. There will be setbacks that feel like the end of the world. There will be people who don't believe in your vision. There will be moments when you question everything you're building.

But here's what I've learned: every breakdown contains the seeds of a breakthrough if you're willing to learn the lesson completely.

Every failure teaches you something you need to know for your next level of success. Every rejection redirects you toward something better aligned with your purpose. Every crisis creates opportunities for people who are prepared to see them.

The question isn't whether you'll face challenges. The question is whether you'll use those challenges as fuel for your growth or excuses for your limitations.

What's Possible for You:

I don't know your specific situation, but I know this: if a girl from Outeast, Jacksonville, who was sexually abused, addicted to the streets, and sitting in prison at 24 can build a multi-million-dollar empire and help thousands of other people transform their lives—then whatever you're facing right now is not the end of your story.

You might be in prison reading this, wondering if transformation is really possible for someone like you. It is.

You might be dancing in clubs, making quick money but knowing it's not sustainable long-term. You can transition.

You might be working multiple jobs, barely paying bills, feeling like you'll never get ahead. You can build wealth.

You might be sitting in a corporate job that's slowly killing your soul, dreaming of starting your own business but scared to take the leap. You can make the jump.

You might be dealing with bad credit, no connections, and a background that makes traditional paths seem impossible. You can create your own path.

I know because I've helped thousands of people do exactly that. I've seen former drug dealers become successful entrepreneurs. I've watched single mothers build six-figure businesses. I've celebrated with formerly incarcerated people who now own their own companies.

Your transformation is not just possible—it's inevitable if you commit to the process.

Your Next Steps:

1. **Choose your first area of focus.** Don't try to transform everything at once. Pick one area—credit repair, business formation, tax planning, skill development—and master it completely.
2. **Invest in your education.** Whether it's my courses, someone else's programs, or just books and YouTube videos—commit to learning something new every day.
3. **Start serving others.** Find ways to help people in your network, even if it's just sharing knowledge you've gained. Service creates opportunities.
4. **Document your journey.** Write down your goals, track your progress, and share your story as you transform. Your journey will inspire others and keep you accountable.

5. **Build your network.** Connect with people who are where you want to be and people who are where you used to be. Serve both groups differently but consistently.

6. **Take imperfect action.** Don't wait until you have it all figured out. Start where you are, with what you have, and improve as you go.

A Personal Invitation:

I want you to know that everything I've built—the courses, the community, the businesses—exists to help people like you make this transformation.

If you're ready to learn the specific strategies I use to help people repair their credit, optimize their taxes, and build legitimate businesses, visit my website at **Iambillionairebarbie.vip.** Follow me on social media @IAmBillionaireBarbie for daily content that will keep you motivated and educated.

Join my Rich Off Taxes Entry Level or VIP Section Communities where you'll connect with other women who are building empires from unconventional backgrounds. Get access to my courses on credit repair, tax planning, and business building.

But most importantly, start believing that you deserve the same success you see other people achieving. Stop thinking that wealth and freedom are reserved for people who didn't make the mistakes you made or come from the places you came from.

The Promise I Made in Prison:

When I was locked up, I promised God that if He gave me another chance, I would use whatever platform I was given to bring others with me. This book is part of fulfilling that promise. Your transformation is part of fulfilling that promise.

When you build wealth, you don't just change your life—you change your family's life, your community's trajectory, and the possibilities for everyone who comes after you.

When you break generational patterns, you're not just escaping your circumstances—you're creating new normals for people who will never know what it felt like to be trapped by the limitations you overcame.

When you share your story of transformation, you're not just celebrating your success—you're giving someone else permission to believe that their transformation is possible too.

Your Future is Waiting:

The woman you're becoming is already proud of the decision you're about to make. The life you're building is already attracting the opportunities you need. The empire you're creating is already generating the wealth that will serve generations.

You just have to choose to step into it.

Your background is not your destiny. Your mistakes are not your identity. Your current circumstances are not your final destination.

You are exactly where you need to be to build exactly what you're meant to build.

The blueprint is in your hands. The choice is yours.

Your empire starts now.

With love and abundance,

Billionaire Barbie

P.S. Remember what I learned in prison: favor isn't fair, but it's real. The favor that's on my life is also available to you. The same God who saved me when I should have gotten 40 years is the same God who will open doors for you when you're walking in purpose.

Claim your favor. Build your empire. Change your world.

YOUR ACTION PLAN: THE NEXT 30 DAYS

Week 1: Foundation

- Write down your current financial situation honestly
- List your skills, even ones from unconventional sources
- Research one area: credit repair, tax planning, or business formation
- Join one online community focused on wealth building

Week 2: Education

- Read one book or take one course on your chosen focus area
- Follow successful people in your field on social media

- Write down 10 specific financial goals with deadlines
- Start documenting your journey daily

Week 3: Implementation

- Take one concrete action toward your biggest goal
- Help someone else with knowledge you already have
- Apply for business license or EIN if starting a business
- Begin improving one aspect of your credit score

Week 4: Acceleration

- Launch your first small income stream
- Connect with 5 new people in your network
- Review and adjust your goals based on what you've learned
- Plan your next 90 days with specific milestones

The 90-Day Blueprint:

- Month 1: Education and foundation building
- Month 2: Implementation and testing
- Month 3: Scaling and optimization

Your transformation doesn't have to take years. It starts with the decision to begin, and it accelerates with consistent daily action.

Start today. Your future self is waiting.

RESOURCES

DAILY AFFIRMATIONS FOR TRANSFORMATION

Read these affirmations daily, preferably in the morning and before bed. Speak them with conviction, feel them in your body, and believe them in your spirit. Your words have power—use them to create the reality you deserve.

Identity & Worth Affirmations

I am more than my past mistakes. My history does not define my destiny. Every day, I am becoming the woman I was meant to be.

I am worthy of wealth, love, and success. I deserve abundance in every area of my life. I release any beliefs that tell me otherwise.

I am a powerful creator of my reality. With my thoughts, words, and actions, I am building the empire of my dreams.

I am exactly where I need to be. Every experience has prepared me for this moment of transformation and growth.

I am breaking generational curses with my choices. I am the ancestor my future generations will thank for changing everything.

Wealth & Abundance Affirmations

Money flows to me easily and abundantly. I am a magnet for financial opportunities. Wealth is my birthright, and I claim it now.

I build multiple streams of income that work without me. My money works harder than I do. I create systems that generate wealth while I sleep.

I think like a billionaire because I am becoming one. Abundance is my natural state. I make decisions from wealth consciousness, not scarcity.

Every dollar I invest in myself returns to me multiplied. My education, my growth, and my development create exponential returns in my life.

I attract clients who are excited to pay me premium prices. People value my expertise and gladly exchange their money for my transformation services.

I always have more money than I need. I cannot help but to attract a lot of money into my life. In Jesus Name Amen!

Business & Success Affirmations

I am a successful entrepreneur who serves and profits. My business helps people transform their lives while creating the wealth I deserve.

I solve problems that people pay me well to solve. My skills, knowledge, and experience are valuable assets that generate consistent income.

I make decisions quickly and adjust as I learn. I trust my intuition and take imperfect action rather than waiting for perfect conditions.

My business grows stronger every day. Each challenge makes me wiser. Each success builds momentum for the next level.

I am building a legacy that outlasts my lifetime. My work creates opportunities for generations of people who come after me.

Mindset & Resilience Affirmations

I see opportunities where others see obstacles. Every crisis contains seeds of breakthrough. I find solutions that others cannot see.

I am resilient, resourceful, and unstoppable. Nothing can keep me down permanently. I rise stronger from every setback.

I trust the process of my transformation. Even when I cannot see the full picture, I know I am being guided toward my highest good.

I release the need to control outcomes. I do my part and trust that favor and divine timing will handle the rest.

I celebrate progress, not just perfection. Every step forward is worthy of acknowledgment. I honor my growth journey.

Relationships & Community Affirmations

I attract people who support my vision and growth. My network is filled with people who believe in me and want to see me win.

I lift others as I climb to my own success. My transformation creates space for other people to transform their lives.

I forgive myself and others for past mistakes. I release resentment and choose love, knowing that forgiveness frees me to move forward.

I communicate with clarity, kindness, and confidence. My words build bridges and create solutions. I speak life into every situation.

I am surrounded by abundance and loving support. The universe conspires to help me succeed. I am never alone in my journey.

Spiritual & Purpose Affirmations

I am walking in my divine purpose. God has equipped me with everything I need to fulfill my mission on this earth.

Favor follows me wherever I go. Doors open for me. Opportunities find me. I am blessed beyond measure.

I trust God's timing and plan for my life. What is meant for me will not pass me by. I surrender control and embrace faith.

I am a vessel for transformation and healing. My story helps others believe that their transformation is possible too.

I use my platform to bring others with me. Success is sweeter when shared. I create opportunities for people who look like me.

Daily Power Statements

Today, I choose abundance over scarcity. Today, I choose action over excuses. Today, I choose growth over comfort. Today, I choose faith over fear. Today, I choose my future over my past.

Morning Intention Setting

Say this each morning before starting your day:

"Today is a gift, and I receive it with gratitude. I am open to opportunities, aligned with my purpose, and ready to serve at my highest level. Money flows to me, favor follows me, and success is inevitable because I am committed to my transformation. I am Billionaire Barbie, and my empire grows stronger with every choice I make. Rich risings and abundant blessings to me and everyone I encounter today."

Evening Gratitude & Preparation

Say this each night before sleep:

"I am grateful for this day and all the lessons it brought. I release any stress, worry, or disappointment from today. I forgive myself for any mistakes and celebrate every victory, no matter how small. As I sleep, my subconscious mind works on my goals, attracting opportunities and solutions while I rest. I trust that tomorrow brings new possibilities for growth, service, and abundance. I am exactly where I need to be, becoming exactly who I am meant to be."

Special Circumstances Affirmations

When Facing Rejection: "This 'no' is redirecting me to something better. What is meant for me cannot miss me."

When Dealing with Setbacks: "This is not happening to me, it is happening for me. I extract the lesson and keep moving forward."

When Feeling Overwhelmed: "I take life one day, one decision, one breath at a time. I am capable of handling whatever comes."

When Doubting Your Worth: "I am worthy because I exist. My value is not determined by my past or my current circumstances."

When Money is Tight: "This is temporary. I am resourceful and creative. Abundance is flowing to me now."

When People Don't Believe in You: "Other people's opinions are not my reality. I believe in myself, and that is enough."

How To Use These Affirmations

1. **Choose 3-5 affirmations** that resonate most with your current situation
2. **Read them aloud** with conviction and emotion
3. **Visualize them** as your current reality while speaking them
4. **Feel the emotions** of already having what you're affirming
5. **Repeat consistently** - morning and evening minimum
6. **Write them down** in your journal or on sticky notes
7. **Adjust as needed** - change affirmations as your life changes

Remember: Affirmations work when combined with aligned action. Speak it, believe it, then do the work to make it reality.

Your words are creating your world. Choose them wisely.

"Life and death are in the power of the tongue. Speak life into your situation, speak abundance into your finances, speak success into your business, and speak transformation into your future."

— **Billionaire Barbie**

BILLIONAIRE BARBIE'S PROGRAMS & SERVICES

Educational Courses

Rich Off Taxes Masterclass

- Comprehensive tax strategy course for business owners
- Learn legal deductions, business structure optimization, and wealth-building tax techniques
- Includes templates, worksheets, and step-by-step implementation guides

Credit Sweep Blueprint

- Complete system for improving credit scores and building business credit
- Covers dispute processes, credit building strategies, and funding opportunities
- Access to templates, letters, and automation tools

Business Formation Bootcamp

- Everything you need to start and structure your business legally

- LLC vs. S-Corp guidance, EIN applications, and banking setup
- Includes state-by-state requirements and compliance checklists

Digital Empire Building

- Learn to create passive income through online courses and digital products
- Social media marketing, content creation, and audience building strategies
- Sales funnel creation and automation systems

Done-For-You Services

Billionaire Luxury Tax Services

- Professional tax preparation and planning
- Business tax optimization and compliance
- Representation for tax issues and audits

Billionaire Business Credit Solutions

- Credit repair and restoration services
- Business credit building and funding assistance
- Personal and business credit monitoring

Business Formation Services

- Complete business setup and registration
- Banking and merchant account assistance
- Ongoing compliance and bookkeeping support

Mentorship & Coaching

Rich Off Taxes Entry Level & VIP Section Communities

- Monthly group coaching calls
- Private Facebook community access
- Networking events and masterminds
- Exclusive content and resources

VIP Mentorship Program

- One-on-one coaching with Billionaire Barbie
- Customized business strategy development
- Direct access for questions and guidance
- Quarterly in-person intensive sessions

Connect with Billionaire Barbie:

- Website: https://iambillionairebarbie.vip/
- Instagram: @IAmBillionaireBarbie
- Facebook: Billionaire Barbie Official
- TikTok: @BillionaireBarbie
- YouTube: Billionaire Barbie TV
- Email: info@billionairebarbie.com

FINANCIAL LITERACY STARTER GUIDE

Understanding Credit Scores

What Affects Your Credit Score:

- Payment history (35% of score)
- Credit utilization (30% of score)
- Length of credit history (15% of score)
- Types of credit accounts (10% of score)
- New credit inquiries (10% of score)

Credit Score Ranges:

- Excellent: 750-850
- Good: 700-749
- Fair: 650-699
- Poor: 600-649
- Bad: Below 600

Quick Credit Improvement Tips:

- Pay all bills on time, every time

- Keep credit card balances below 30% of limits
- Don't close old credit accounts
- Limit new credit applications
- Monitor your credit report regularly

Basic Tax Deductions for Entrepreneurs

Home Office Deduction:

- Percentage of home used exclusively for business
- Utilities, rent/mortgage interest, repairs proportionally deductible

Vehicle Expenses:

- Mileage method: Standard IRS rate per business mile
- Actual expense method: Percentage of total vehicle costs

Business Equipment:

- Computers, phones, software subscriptions
- Office furniture and supplies
- Professional development and education

Marketing and Advertising:

- Website development and maintenance
- Social media advertising
- Business cards, flyers, promotional materials

Professional Services:

- Legal fees, accounting services
- Business consultations and coaching
- Professional memberships and subscriptions

Business Structure Basics

Sole Proprietorship:

- Simplest structure, no separate business entity
- Personal liability for business debts
- Income reported on personal tax return

LLC (Limited Liability Company):

- Personal asset protection from business liabilities
- Flexible tax options (sole proprietor, partnership, or corporation)
- Minimal paperwork and maintenance requirements

S-Corporation:

- Potential tax savings on self-employment taxes
- Must pay reasonable salary to owner-employees
- More complex bookkeeping and reporting requirements

C-Corporation:

- Complete separation between personal and business
- Double taxation on profits and dividends
- Best for companies seeking investment or going public

VISUALIZATION EXERCISES

Daily Abundance Visualization (10 minutes)

1. **Set the Scene** (2 minutes)
    - o Find quiet space, close eyes, take deep breaths
    - o Clear your mind of daily distractions
2. **Create Your Future Reality** (5 minutes)
    - o Visualize your ideal day 5 years from now
    - o See yourself in your dream home, driving your dream car
    - o Feel the emotions of financial freedom and success
    - o Experience helping others transform their lives
3. **Engage All Senses** (2 minutes)
    - o What do you see, hear, smell, touch, taste?
    - o Make the vision as real as possible
    - o Feel gratitude for this future reality
4. **Anchor the Vision** (1 minute)
    - o Take three deep breaths
    - o Set intention for one action you'll take today
    - o Open eyes and write down key insights

Goal Manifestation Technique

The Prison Method (Billionaire Barbie's Technique):

1. Write your goal in present tense as if it's already achieved
2. Include specific details: dates, amounts, emotions
3. Read it every morning and night
4. Visualize it happening for 5 minutes daily
5. Take aligned action toward the goal consistently
6. Adjust and update as you grow

Example Goal Statement: "It is December 31, 2025, and I am celebrating my first $100,000 year in my credit repair business. I feel proud, accomplished, and grateful as I help my 500th client improve their financial situation. My family is secure, my bills are paid in advance, and I'm planning our vacation to celebrate this milestone."

Weekly Vision Board Exercise

Digital Vision Board Creation:

- Use Pinterest, Canva, or vision board apps
- Include images of your goals: home, car, lifestyle, business
- Add inspiring quotes and affirmations
- Set as phone/computer wallpaper
- Update monthly as goals evolve

Physical Vision Board Process:

- Gather magazines, printouts, art supplies
- Create collage representing your ideal life

- Place where you'll see it daily
- Spend 5 minutes daily looking at and feeling your vision
- Add new images as dreams expand

RECOMMENDED READING

Personal Development & Mindset

- **"Think and Grow Rich" by Napoleon Hill** - Classic wealth mindset principles
- **"The 7 Habits of Highly Effective People" by Stephen Covey** - Personal effectiveness strategies
- **"Abundance is Your Birthright" by Ash Cash** - Growth vs. fixed mindset concepts
- **"The Power of Now" by Eckhart Tolle** - Present moment awareness and peace

Business & Entrepreneurship

- **"The Lean Startup" by Eric Ries** - Modern business building methodology
- **"The $100 Startup" by Chris Guillebeau** - Start business with minimal investment
- **"Profit First" by Mike Michalowicz** - Financial management for small businesses
- **"The E-Myth Revisited" by Michael Gerber** - Working on vs. in your business

Financial Literacy & Wealth Building

- **"Rich Dad Poor Dad" by Robert Kiyosaki** - Financial education basics
- **"You Deserve to Be Rich" by Earn Your Leisure** - Real wealth building habits
- **"Abundance Formula" by Ash Cash & Amina Phelps** - Practical money management
- **"The Total Money Makeover" by Dave Ramsey** - Debt elimination strategies

Credit & Real Estate

- **"Credit Repair Kit for Dummies" by Steve Bucci** - DIY credit improvement
- **"The Book on Rental Property Investing" by Brandon Turner** - Real estate investing basics
- **"Your Score" by Anthony Davenport** - Advanced credit strategies

Inspiration & Biography

- **"Becoming" by Michelle Obama** - Overcoming obstacles and finding purpose
- **"The Autobiography of Malcolm X"** - Transformation and personal growth
- **"Long Walk to Freedom" by Nelson Mandela** - Resilience and leadership
- **"Born a Crime" by Trevor Noah** - Rising above difficult circumstances

BUSINESS STARTUP CHECKLIST

Legal Foundation

- ☐ Choose business structure (LLC, Corporation, etc.)
- ☐ Register business name with state
- ☐ Obtain federal EIN (Employer Identification Number)
- ☐ Get required licenses and permits
- ☐ Register for state and local taxes
- ☐ Obtain business insurance

Financial Setup

- ☐ Open business checking account
- ☐ Apply for business credit card
- ☐ Set up bookkeeping system (QuickBooks, etc.)
- ☐ Establish business credit profile
- ☐ Create business budget and financial projections
- ☐ Set up payment processing (PayPal, Stripe, Square)

Operations

- ☐ Create business plan and mission statement
- ☐ Develop products or services offerings

- [ ] Set pricing strategy
- [ ] Create standard operating procedures
- [ ] Establish supplier relationships
- [ ] Set up business location/workspace

Marketing & Sales

- [ ] Build professional website
- [ ] Set up social media profiles
- [ ] Create marketing materials
- [ ] Develop content strategy
- [ ] Establish customer acquisition plan
- [ ] Create sales process and tracking system

Technology & Tools

- [ ] Purchase necessary equipment and software
- [ ] Set up customer management system (CRM)
- [ ] Establish email marketing platform
- [ ] Create file organization system
- [ ] Set up project management tools
- [ ] Implement security measures

EMERGENCY CONTACTS & RESOURCES

Legal Help

- **SCORE Mentors** - Free business mentoring: www.score.org
- **Small Business Administration (SBA)** - Government support: www.sba.gov
- **Legal Aid Society** - Free/low-cost legal services
- **Local Bar Association** - Attorney referrals

Financial Assistance

- **211** - Dial 2-1-1 for local assistance programs
- **Salvation Army** - Emergency financial help
- **Catholic Charities** - Financial and social services
- **United Way** - Community support programs

Credit & Debt Help

- **National Foundation for Credit Counseling** - www.nfcc.org

- **Consumer Financial Protection Bureau** - www.consumer-finance.gov
- **Annual Credit Report** - www.annualcreditreport.com (free reports)

Mental Health & Support

- **National Suicide Prevention Lifeline** - 988
- **Crisis Text Line** - Text HOME to 741741
- **SAMHSA National Helpline** - 1-800-662-4357
- **Psychology Today** - Find therapists: www.psychologytoday.com

Reentry Support

- **National Reentry Resource Center** - www.nationalreentryresourcecenter.org
- **Center for Employment Opportunities** - www.ceoworks.org
- **The Last Mile** - www.thelastmile.org

Remember: Your transformation is not just possible—it's inevitable when you commit to the process and take consistent action. Use these resources as stepping stones to build the empire you deserve.

Rich Risings and Abundant Blessings, Billionaire Barbie

A LETTER TO WOMEN
WHO FEEL STUCK

My beautiful sister,

I'm writing this letter specifically to you—the woman who picked up this book because something inside you knows you're meant for more, but you can't figure out how to get there from where you are right now.

Maybe you're reading this in a prison cell, counting down days and wondering if transformation is really possible for someone with your record. Maybe you're getting ready for another shift at a club, making money that feels good in the moment but knowing deep down it's not sustainable. Maybe you're working multiple jobs, barely keeping your head above water, watching other people build wealth while you struggle to pay bills.

Or maybe you're in a corporate office, making decent money but feeling like your soul is dying a little more each day, knowing you have gifts and dreams you're not using but scared to take the leap.

Wherever you are, whatever your situation, I need you to know something: I see you. I've been you. And I'm writing this letter to tell you that where you are right now is not where you have to stay.

You Are Not Broken

First, let me destroy a lie that society has probably been telling you your whole life: there is nothing wrong with you that needs to be fixed.

You are not broken because you made survival choices in desperate situations. You are not damaged goods because you used the only resources you had available at the time. You are not less valuable because your path looks different from what's considered "normal."

The same strength that got you through your darkest moments is the same strength that will build your empire. The same resourcefulness that helped you survive is the same resourcefulness that will make you wealthy. The same resilience that kept you going when everything fell apart is the same resilience that will carry you to levels of success that will shock the people who counted you out.

Your background is not a liability—it's an asset waiting to be leveraged.

Your Pain Has Purpose

I know it might be hard to believe right now, but everything you've been through has been preparing you for something bigger than you can imagine.

The abuse taught you about the importance of boundaries and protecting others from predators. The poverty taught you about resourcefulness and the value of money. The mistakes taught you about consequences and the importance of making better choices. The trauma taught you about healing and the power of transformation.

None of it was wasted. None of it was meaningless. All of it—every tear, every struggle, every moment you thought you wouldn't make it—has been building your capacity to help others overcome similar challenges.

Your mess is going to become your message. Your wounds are going to become your wisdom. Your testimony is going to become someone else's roadmap to freedom.

But first, you have to stop running from your story and start running with it.

You Have Everything You Need

I know it doesn't feel like it, but you already possess everything you need to transform your life completely.

You have intelligence—maybe not the kind that shows up on school tests, but the kind that helped you navigate complex situations and read people's intentions. Street smarts, survival instincts, and intuitive wisdom are forms of intelligence that business schools can't teach.

You have strength—you're still here despite everything that tried to break you. That's not luck; that's power. That's resilience. That's the raw material that empires are built from.

You have experience—you understand struggle in ways that privileged people never will. You know what it feels like to be counted out, overlooked, and underestimated. That perspective is valuable. That authenticity is rare. That credibility is priceless.

You have stories—not just the painful ones, but the triumph ones too. Every time you got back up, every time you chose to try again, every time you helped someone else despite your own struggles. Those stories will inspire and transform other people's lives.

You have gifts—talents, abilities, and perspectives that the world needs. They might be buried under years of trauma and survival mode, but they're there. Your job is to uncover them, develop them, and use them to serve others while building your own wealth.

Permission to Dream Again

Maybe it's been so long since you allowed yourself to dream that you've forgotten how. Maybe you've been in survival mode for so long that thinking beyond next week feels impossible. Maybe you've been disappointed so many times that hope feels dangerous.

I'm giving you permission to dream again.

Not small dreams. Not "realistic" dreams that fit other people's expectations of what's possible for someone like you. Big, bold, audacious dreams that make you feel excited and terrified at the same time.

Dream about the business you'll build. Dream about the house you'll buy. Dream about the generational wealth you'll create. Dream about the lives you'll change. Dream about the legacy you'll leave.

And then write those dreams down. Make them real on paper. Give them shape and substance and deadlines. Because dreams without plans are just wishes, but dreams with plans become goals, and goals with action become reality.

You Don't Have to Have It All Figured Out

One of the biggest lies that keeps women stuck is the belief that you need to know exactly how you're going to achieve your goals before you start working toward them.

That's not how transformation works. That's not how business works. That's not how life works.

You just need to know your next step. One step. One decision. One action that moves you closer to where you want to be.

Maybe that step is getting your GED. Maybe it's taking a course on credit repair. Maybe it's starting a small business with the skills you already have. Maybe it's having an honest conversation with someone who can help you. Maybe it's applying for a job that seems just out of reach.

You don't need to see the whole staircase—you just need to take the first step. The next step will reveal itself when you're ready for it.

Your Timeline is Your Timeline

Social media will try to convince you that if you haven't "made it" by a certain age, you've missed your window. That's a lie designed to keep you small.

I didn't start building legitimate wealth until my thirties. I didn't discover my true calling until after I'd failed at several other things. I didn't become the woman I am today until I'd been through everything I needed to go through to become her.

Your transformation doesn't have an expiration date. Your potential doesn't decrease with age. Your ability to start over doesn't diminish because of how many times you've started over before.

Whether you're 18 or 58, whether this is your first attempt at change or your fifteenth, whether you're starting with $5 or $5,000—if you're breathing, you have time to build something beautiful.

Stop comparing your chapter 3 to someone else's chapter 20. Focus on your own story, your own pace, your own journey.

Find Your People

One of the hardest parts of transformation is doing it alone. You need people who believe in your vision even when you're struggling to believe in it yourself. You need people who see your potential even when you can't see it. You need people who will celebrate your wins and support you through your losses.

Those people might not be your family. They might not be your current friends. They might not be people who knew you before you decided to change.

That's okay. Family isn't just about blood—it's about bond. It's about shared vision and mutual support and unconditional love. Build a chosen family of people who want to see you win.

Look for women who are where you want to be and learn from them. Look for women who are where you used to be and help them. Surround yourself with people who speak life into your dreams instead of death into your potential.

Join communities, take courses, attend events, engage on social media—do whatever it takes to find your tribe. Your network will become your net worth, but more importantly, your community will become your strength.

Forgive Yourself

This might be the hardest part, but it's also the most necessary part: you have to forgive yourself for the choices you made when you didn't know better, when you didn't have better options, when you were operating from pain instead of purpose.

Forgive yourself for the time you feel like you wasted. Forgive yourself for the opportunities you missed. Forgive yourself for the people you hurt, including yourself. Forgive yourself for not being where you think you should be by now.

That forgiveness isn't about excusing harmful behavior or avoiding accountability. It's about releasing the shame and guilt that will sabotage your success if you carry them with you.

You cannot build a beautiful future on a foundation of self-hatred. You cannot create abundance from a place of self-condemnation. You cannot help other people heal if you refuse to heal yourself.

Forgiveness is not a feeling—it's a decision. Decide to forgive yourself, and then choose that decision over and over again until it becomes your reality.

Your Success is Inevitable

I need you to understand something: when you commit fully to your transformation, when you do the internal work and take consistent external action, when you refuse to give up no matter what obstacles arise—your success becomes inevitable.

Not easy. Not immediate. Not without challenges and setbacks and moments when you want to quit. But inevitable.

Because you have something that people who've never struggled don't have: the knowledge that rock bottom is a solid foundation to build on. You've already survived the worst things you thought could happen to you. Everything else is just problem-solving.

You have something that people who've never failed don't have: the humility to keep learning, the hunger to keep growing, and the appreciation for every blessing that comes your way.

You have something that people who've never been counted out don't have: the fire in your belly that comes from proving everyone wrong who said you'd never amount to anything.

That fire is your superpower. That hunger is your advantage. That strength is your guarantee.

The World Needs What You Have

Finally, and most importantly, I need you to know that your transformation isn't just about you. It's about every little girl who needs to see that someone who looks like her, who comes from where she comes from, can build something beautiful from nothing.

It's about every woman who's making the same mistakes you used to make, who needs to hear your story so she can believe that change is possible.

It's about every person who's been told they're not smart enough, not good enough, not worthy enough to achieve their dreams, who needs to see you winning so they can give themselves permission to win too.

The world needs your transformation. Your community needs your success. Your family needs your breakthrough. Your future children and grandchildren need the foundation you're going to build.

You are not just changing your life—you are changing your lineage. You are not just building wealth—you are building hope. You are not just healing yourself—you are healing everyone who comes after you.

Your Time is Now

Sister, I don't know what brought you to this book, but I know it wasn't an accident. You picked up this book because something inside you is ready to change everything. That something is your time arriving.

Your past is your power. Your future is your choice. Your transformation starts the moment you decide it starts.

Stop waiting for permission. Stop waiting for perfect conditions. Stop waiting for someone to come save you.

Save yourself. Build yourself. Create yourself.

The blueprint is in your hands. The choice is yours. The time is now.

Your empire is waiting for you to claim it.

With infinite love and unshakeable faith in your transformation,

Billionaire Barbie

P.S. Remember: You are not reading this by accident. You are reading this because you are ready. Trust that readiness. Act on that readiness. Your future self is already proud of what you're about to do.

If You Need Immediate Support

Crisis Support:

- National Suicide Prevention Lifeline: 988
- Crisis Text Line: Text HOME to 741741

Financial Emergency:

- Dial 211 for local assistance programs
- Salvation Army: 1-800-728-7825

Domestic Violence:

- National Domestic Violence Hotline: 1-800-799-7233

Substance Abuse:

- SAMHSA National Helpline: 1-800-662-4357

You are not alone. Help is available. Hope is real. Your transformation is possible.

www.ingramcontent.com/pod-product-compliance
Lightning Source LLC
Chambersburg PA
CBHW060150130626
46556CB00006B/2575